D1094587

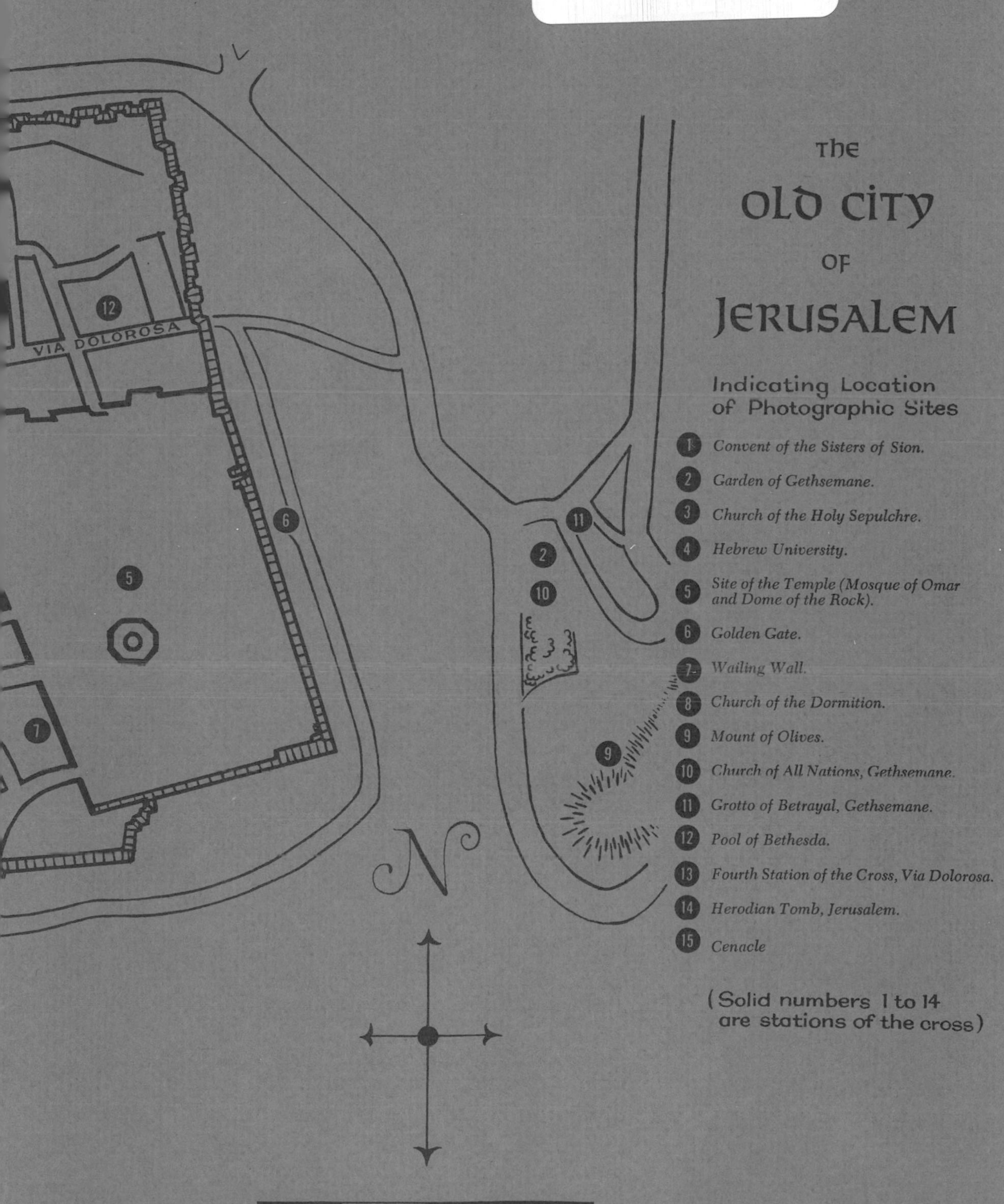
The
OLD CITY
OF
JERUSALEM
Indicating Location of Photographic Sites
1 Convent of the Sisters of Sion.
2 Garden of Gethsemane.
3 Church of the Holy Sepulchre.
4 Hebrew University.
5 Site of the Temple (Mosque of Omar and Dome of the Rock).
6 Golden Gate.
7 Wailing Wall.
8 Church of the Dormition.
9 Mount of Olives.
10 Church of All Nations, Gethsemane.
11 Grotto of Betrayal, Gethsemane.
12 Pool of Bethesda.
13 Fourth Station of the Cross, Via Dolorosa.
14 Herodian Tomb, Jerusalem.
15 Cenacle
(Solid numbers 1 to 14 are stations of the cross)
VIA DOLOROSA
N
0
110
220
440
Scale in yards

This is
THE HOLY LAND

The Old City of Jerusalem from the roof of the Convent of the Sisters of Zion

Church of the Visitation, Ain Karem

Star of Bethlehem, Grotto of the Nativity, Church of the Nativity, Bethlehem

Bethlehem

Loaves and fishes, Tabgha, Sea of Galilee

Mount of Beatitudes, overlooking Sea of Galilee and Plain of Genezereth

Garden of Gethsemane, Jerusalem

Chapel of the
Nailing to the Cross,
Mount Calvary,
Church of the
Holy Sepulchre,
Jerusalem

Holy Sepulchre,
Church of the
Holy Sepulchre,
Jerusalem

This is the holy land

A PILGRIMAGE IN
WORDS AND PICTURES

CONDUCTED BY FULTON J. SHEEN
PHOTOGRAPHED BY YOUSUF KARSH
DESCRIBED BY H. V. MORTON

WITH A FOREWORD BY
BISHOP SHEEN

HAWTHORN BOOKS, INC.

PUBLISHERS · NEW YORK

 This book was manufactured in the United States and published simultaneously in Canada by McClelland & Stewart, Ltd., 25 Hollinger Road, Toronto 16. Library of Congress Catalogue Card Number 61-6706. Dewey Decimal Classification 915.69

First Edition, March 1961

Nihil Obstat

JOSEPH H. BRADY, S.T.D.
CENSOR LIBRORUM

Imprimatur

THOMAS A. BOLAND, S.T.D.
ARCHBISHOP OF NEWARK

October 25, 1960

CONTENTS

Bethany, home of Martha, Mary and Lazarus

A FOREWORD

by The Most Reverend Fulton J. Sheen, D.D., PH.D.

IN PERIODS of human strife, when world wars come within two decades of one another, when men cease to be men and begin to act like beasts—there is a peculiar perversity which makes them abnormally interested in their bestial origin. Hence, the joy of finding a primitive tool, a club with which the first cave man beat the first cave woman and dragged her by her hair to his lair; hence, the relish of discovering the markings of a claw, or a tentacle on an earthen floor, or the vision of a fossil skull, or the tracings of a reindeer on a wall. Like a poor man rejoicing in discovering that he has rich relatives, some exult in tracing their biological lineage back again to "nature, in tooth and claw."

But as man advances in morality away from the barbarian and the shedding of his brother's blood, he becomes interested in another genealogy——the bonds that tie him not to the beast but to God. The quest of this kind of a missing link becomes a passion.

It was this quest for our origins that drove my two grandnephews, Jerry and Fulton Cunningham, to go in search of caves. Perhaps in cellars under the floor of the world, we would find traces of that God-likeness which makes a man more than a man.

We started out for what used to be known as Palestine and we found out that the world was both right and wrong. Right, in that we came from the Cave Man; wrong, in that His Name was Christ, not Pithecanthropus; right, in that there were traces of animals in the caves, but they were not reindeer and wolves, but an ox and an ass; right, in that there was a cave man and a cave woman; wrong, in that it was not one who clubbed the other, but rather unfriendly neighbors who clubbed both by slamming the door of an inn in their faces.

What we found was not the beast under the earth, but heaven under the earth; not the man in the tree, but the Man on the Tree—— "The Son of the Most High."

What we learned was that whenever one wants to rediscover something of the Life of Christ, one has to stoop——and the stoop is the sign of humility. If you insist on drawing yourself up to your full height, you are denied entrance to the scene of a mystery. "The man who does not accept the kingdom of God like a little child, will not enter into it." Even the church door at Bethlehem is so low one has to surrender the pride of height to enter. The place of the crib, the scene of the Visitation, where Mary visited her aged cousin, Elizabeth; the birthplace of John the Baptist; the home at Nazareth—all are humiliating to human pride. Our Lord seemed always to be under the earth as the Heavenly Atlas in order to lift it up, always under the level of man to carry him to the Throne man lost when he gave up a garden for a fruit.

When we consider greater areas, there are still depths. Our Lord's public ministry, for the most part, was spent around the shore of Galilee which is about 680 feet below the level of the sea. Jericho, where He was a guest of Zacchaeus, is a city of depths. If we dig deep enough we find traces of a civilization going back to 2000 B.C.

There were heights, of course, but even the heights were depths, for they were the parading of humiliation——the Mount of the Temptation, where the devil asked Him to take three short cuts from the Cross; the Mount of Transfiguration where He spoke to Moses and Elias of His Death; Calvary where He was unfurled as a Man Who lost the Battle to win the Victory. Even the Hill of Beatitudes was the prelude to the Hill of Calvary, for He Who refused to glorify publicity, sex, money, self-expression, wrote His own sentence of death.

Not until one looks at the Land called "Holy" does one understand that line of Paul about Christ:

> He dispossessed Himself and took the nature of a slave, fashioned in the likeness of men, and presenting Himself to us in human form.

The Greek word for this dispossession is *kenosis,* which also means an "emptying," a beclouding of glory such as a King becoming a servant. This emptying is found even in the land that He chose for His human Birth. Politically, it was an enslaved nation; economically, it was poor. The very ground itself also seemed as if it were stoned from heaven. The Rabbis used to say that "when God made the world, He had two bags of stones; one He scattered all over the world and the other He dropped on Palestine."

But the emptying was not only in the land in which He became Incarnate, but in His companions, for the most part ignorant fishermen. His was not the kind of intellectual recreation the wise men of Rome or Greece would have sought.

The two boys and I took three kinds of baggage with us, without which one cannot see the Holy Land. Some people carry only two kinds. Our three were eyes, memory and faith. Eyes took in the sights, but the eyes of a bird could see them better. Memory is history, the knowledge that one has of the successive layers of civilization which the learned can peel off stratum by stratum until the core is reached.

But most important of all is faith, for faith is another pair of eyes, a kind of X-ray which penetrates beneath the surface and sees the meaning of it all. The boys had good eyes; also an unusual amount of memory for their ages because they had read much. But, above all, they had faith, which was like a telescope to the eyes and an interpreter for memory.

The eyes of the young see more than the eyes of the old, not because they are young, but because they light up. There is a primitive,

original quality about the surprise in their eyes at seeing novel sights. They were told they would be disappointed because Calvary is no longer a hill but a church, because the streets of Jerusalem no longer bore the marks of a dragged Cross. But they who read this book will be disappointed that they were not disappointed. In my "Afterword" this will be made even clearer.

Jerry was my server in *This Is the Mass;* then he became my companion in *This Is Rome.* It has been said that all roads lead to Rome, but it has never been said that the reason all roads lead to Rome is because they all start with Jerusalem. For this pilgrimage, we added Jerry's younger brother, Fulton. As I walked with them through the streets of Jerusalem, ever in wonder and astonishment, I well understood the words of Our Lord, "if they keep silence, the stones will cry out instead."

The Gospel comes alive in such a visit. One sees that the only biblical scholars who could ever deny that the Gospels were written by eyewitnesses, or by those who lived in Palestine, would be critics who never visited the land where the Feet of the Lord have walked.

Take, for example, the Resurrection scene. How many of us have pictured the stone in front of the tomb Our Lord was buried in on Good Friday, as round like a ball and something quite distinct from the tomb itself? But what do the Gospels say? When the holy women came to the tomb early on Easter morn, "they began to question among themselves, Who is to roll the stone away from the door of the tomb?" It was not a crude stone at all. It was rather like a mill stone, very wide in circumference and about nine inches in thickness. In the tombs of the rich—and the place where Our Lord was buried was the tomb of the rich man, Joseph of Arimathea—this stone was placed upright in front of the door. When not in use the stone was rolled into a groove cut into the wall. To seal the tomb, the stone was literally "rolled" in front of it. When we saw such a tomb that had belonged to Herod's family, Easter morn came back again.

Sometimes we sat and peeled off layers of history from a sight before us, such as the Mosque of Omar and the adjoining Dome of the Rock. In our mind's eye, we stripped off the Moslem dome and saw the Temple from which the Lord drove the buyers and sellers and in which He called Himself the true Temple because the Temple is where God dwells. We could look up at the opposite hill and see in our mind's eye Vespasian and Titus coming down with their thundering legions, so as not to leave "a stone upon a stone."

More mental excavation and we were back in history to the cave of Ornan the Jebusite, to which David came during the plague and promised to build a Temple to God. David did not seem so far back as we walked the stone floor which David refused to accept as a gift because he would not make an offering to God that was without cost. Then another layer was peeled off and lo, we were back to Mount Moriah, for in the center of the Temple that Solomon built, and still in the center of the Dome of the Rock, was the stone on which Abraham was about to sacrifice his son, Isaac, as a figure of the Father Who would send His only-begotten Son for the Redemption of the world.

Something else came alive at the place where the Lord raised Lazarus from the dead. A slingshot played a very important role in history—and who is the boy that does not love a slingshot? One day we were out in Bethany. A peddler came along selling slingshots. It was not like our Western ones in which two pieces of rubber are attached to either end of a two-pronged fork or crotch cut from a tree. What interested the boys was the shape of it——it was made of a small piece of cloth to which were attached from either end two long strings. The stone was put into the cloth; the sling was then swung around the head; and, finally, when great momentum was generated, one end of the string was released allowing the stone to be thrown a vaster distance than by our rubber slings.

The boys first had an interest only in its shape. Then suddenly it became alive, as we told them that that was the way that David slew Goliath. David took a stone and "shot it from his sling with a whirl so dextrous that it struck Goliath on his forehead; and he fell, face downwards to the earth." It was then that Jerry asked: "Was not that a symbol of Our Lord the King slaying the powers of evil?" Only faith asks such questions.

In the Sermon on the Mount there are eight "Woes" and there are eight Beatitudes. But outside of those "Woes" there were others pro-

Tomb of Lazarus, Bethany

nounced over certain cities along the Sea of Galilee. Here was another example of the Gospel coming alive. I recalled to the boys the Woe of Our Lord over Corozain, Bethsaida and Capharnaum:

> Woe to thee Corozain; woe to thee Bethsaida; and thou Capharnaum, thou shalt fall as low as hell. And I say thus, that it shall go less hard with the country of Sodom on the day of Judgment than with thee.

Not one of these cities over which the denouncement was hurled, survives today; they have all perished and vanished under the impact of Divine Judgment. I asked the boys why Capharnaum in a special way should have been so severely judged by Our Divine Master. Their correct answer was: "Because Our Lord left Nazareth to make Capharnaum His own city and the city rejected Him."

The ruins of the synagogue in Capharnaum were most fascinating. Many stones became as pages through which we taught catechism to the young. One of the stones showed a carving of the Ark of the Covenant on wheels. Having already learned much about the Ark in the desert Tabernacle, as well as in the early Temple of Jerusalem, they were curious as to why it should be pictured on wheels, since it was in a fixed place in the Tabernacle and Temple. The reason, of course, was to describe a particular moment in the history of the Ark. The ark was seized by the Philistines, who put it in the temple of the false Dagon. The next morning Dagon had fallen on his face. Then came a plague, and more troubles. The Philistines wondered if their disasters were due to the God of Israel. They hit upon a test. They took two cows who had little calves and hitched the cows to a wagon in which was the ark. They set the cows in the direction of Israel. The Philistines knew very well that mother cows would not leave their calves; hence, if they ignored their instinct and went straight toward the camp of the Jews, they would then assume that the God of Israel was behind all the trouble. Sacred Scripture says: "The heifers went straight along the road . . . without swerving to right or left; lowing for their calves, but going on still."

The Gospel again came to life in Cana, where Our Lord worked

His first Miracle, and where in the language of Crashaw, "The unconscious waters saw their God and blushed."

When the miraculous wine that had been changed from water was brought to the steward of the feast, "he did not know whence it came; only the servants who had drawn the water knew that." Why did not the steward know, whereas the servants did?

The explanation lies in the fact that the house of Cana had two floors—the lower floor was a kind of basement in which was located the well or cistern. The servants down below, at the suggestion of Our Lord, filled the water pots and then carried them upstairs to the master of the feast. The wine steward did not see the water poured in, but only the new wine, which was changed mysteriously as it was brought up to him. That is why "he did not know whence it came."

When we went to the Mount of Beatitudes we found a group of Spanish pilgrims who asked me to recount for them the Sermon on the Mount and also to relate the incidents which happened below on the lake. One of the pictures in this book depicts that scene.

It is impossible to realize how unworthy one feels to stand in the same spot as the Creator of the World made flesh and to recite His Words. But why should I scruple at geographical identity? Should I not more be chagrined at being His bishop and His priest?

During that Sermon on the Mount, He knew in His Divine Mind that there were murderers, thieves, harlots, intelligentsia, gangsters, juvenile delinquents, before Him. That is why to some He warned of judgment; to the adulterers, He said that looking on a woman and lusting after her was accounted as the deed; to those who paraded their religion, He trumpeted a warning to pray in secret and not for show. There must have been thirty or forty different categories of people in that audience, and he touched every single one of them. It was probably the most personal sermon that was ever given——and that is why there is a connection between the Mount of Beatitudes and the Mount of Calvary. When He crucified the world with His Wisdom, the world resolved to crucify Him. He Who had climbed the Hill of the Beatitudes to be denounced by the world would one day be forced by the world to climb that other Hill on the Friday called Good.

There were also many other striking coincidences. One of them was along the Sea of Galilee at the point where Our Lord, after the Resurrection, prolonged His office of Shepherd to Peter as the shepherd of the Church. Peter was told by the Eternal Rock, Who made Peter the rock of His Church, to feed His lambs and His sheep. This spot is particularly appealing to a bishop or a priest who is summoned to be a shepherd. The day we were there, a shepherd, whose flock was nearby, brought a three-day-old lamb and put it into my hands at the very spot where the Master said: "Feed my lambs." The picture of that scene is also in this book. It made me wonder why one does not love all people who are supposed to be lambs as much as one loved that lamb.

Two other coincidences took place there. After the Resurrection, Our Lord appeared on the shore to the Apostles who were fishing. He had prepared a fire on which He was cooking fish and nearby were loaves of bread. The day we were on that spot, a fisherman had a fire cooking fish with loaves of bread nearby. The fisherman, who might have been another Peter or Andrew, James or John, showed us a fish he caught—a fish called the *musht*. It was not large, but it had a particularly large mouth. Tradition has it that this was the kind of fish which swallowed the coin which Peter extracted to pay his taxes.

When we were at the Jordan, the boys asked if its water could be used to baptize a little brother or sister they were expecting. "How wonderful," they said, "to have water that washed Our Lord wash a baby." When the baby came, whose name is now Paul, he was baptized with that water. Perhaps some day if this series of books continues we may have Paul in pictures in a book called, *This Is Paul's Journey*.

There is no need to tell more. H. V. Morton can tell it better; and Yousuf Karsh can depict it better. It has been said, if you want to know a person, travel a long journey with him. We traveled twice with both of them and there are only two forgotten words to describe them both, "noble gentlemen."

The last picture in the book is that of the boys with the medals given to them by the Franciscans to testify that they made a pilgrimage to the Holy Land. Crusaders fought to go there; saints prayed to go there; repentant sinners yearned to go there. While other boys want to go in space ships to the sun, stars and moon, these boys wanted to see the scenes where a Lady lived who had the moon under her feet, and the twelve apostles as stars about her heart, and the sun, who is the Son of God, above her head.

PRELUDE

WE SAW a small airport upon an ageless landscape. The dusty road that approached it slipped away into the stony hills and the clumps of scarlet poppies. We noticed also a transport plane whose markings proved that this land had attracted the attention of the United Nations.

A group of Arabs, some wearing biblical-looking robes, others in European suits, started up American cars and glanced speculatively towards the approaching passengers. A priest led his pilgrims to them, and upon every face could be read the bewilderment of those who in a few flying hours had exchanged the familiarity of home for the Hashemite Kingdom of Jordan.

"Oh look!" cried both boys together. "Camels!"

And, following their pointing fingers, we saw a file of those supercilious creatures undulating past the United Nations aircraft, forming for a brief moment a strange conjunction which linked the world of today with that of Abraham. Some miles away, upon a mountainous ridge, a gray city, the color of the stones and the rocks, treeless and uncompromising even at that distance, lifted its domes and towers to the sky.

"What's that?" the boys asked.

"That," replied the Bishop, "is Jerusalem."

So began another pilgrimage to the Holy Land.

Jerusalem in the time of Christ, Franciscan Museum, Via Dolorosa, Jerusalem

I

The holy places

THE COUNTRY once known as Palestine, and now divided between the Arab state of Jordan and the Jewish state of Israel, has attracted the Christian pilgrim for more than seventeen centuries. The importance of this land in the history of western civilization bears no relation to its size. At no time during His recorded journeys was Jesus ever more than a hundred and thirty miles from Jerusalem, in a country whose area was roughly about that of New Hampshire or Vermont. This tiny country has become embroidered, as it were, by the piety of Christians; and there is no place or incident mentioned in the Gospels which has not been enshrined by the Latin or the Oriental Churches.

Most of the sites are of immemorial antiquity and surpassing interest; others are perhaps chiefly remarkable for the devotion they have inspired. Who was the first Christian pilgrim? When did he visit the Holy Land? What was the world like in his time?

Questions such as these may pass through the mind of the thoughtful pilgrim today, as he is conducted here and there upon well-worn paths which were beaten out centuries ago. Indeed, so well established are the roads of pilgrimage that many a modern man must feel that, in making the round of the holy sites, he is taking his place in an historical procession whose leaders are lost to sight in the hazy reaches of time: and when the history of Christian pilgrimage is examined, a number of surprising discoveries are made. Pilgrims began to arrive in the Holy Land in the heyday of the Roman Empire, a good century before Christianity was a tolerated religion; and more surprising still, the first pilgrims, though so much closer to the Apostolic Age, saw less in the Holy Land than the pilgrim of today.

Mount of Temptation, near Jericho

The first recorded pilgrim was Alexander, who lived during the reign of the Emperor Septimius Severus, whose triumphal arch is one of the great features of the Forum in Rome. He had been imprisoned in A.D. 204, and had had a dream which caused him to make a vow that he would one day visit Jerusalem, "for the sake of prayer and to obtain knowledge of the Holy Places by enquiry." This devout and scholarly traveler was unable to make his journey until A.D. 212.

The city he saw bore no outward resemblance to the Jerusalem of the Gospels: that city had been entirely destroyed by Titus in A.D. 70, after the Jewish War. The prophecy had been fulfilled. Jesus said, "Do you see all this? . . . there will not be a stone left on another in this place, it will all be thrown down." Upon the site of Jerusalem now rose a Roman city of the time of Hadrian (A.D. 136), named Aelia Capitolina. Like most of the Hellenistic cities of the Near East, its main street was a splendid avenue of columns ("the road called Straight Street," in Damascus, was another), which crossed the city and terminated in a temple of Venus. This seems to have been an enormous circular structure, planted with a grove of trees. Beneath the temple of Venus were concealed the Holy Sepulchre and the Rock of Calvary.

When he went to Bethlehem, Alexander saw that the Grotto of the Nativity had been concealed beneath a temple of Adonis. Thus the first recorded pilgrim was unable to make his devotions at the two chief shrines in the Holy Land. We do not know what other sites were visited by Alexander, but we know that he found a peaceful Christian community living in Aelia Capitolina, under a bishop named Narcissus, who is said to have reached the age of a hundred and sixteen years. That venerable man chose Alexander to be his coadjutor, and after his death the younger man succeeded him as sole bishop. He is the first recorded Christian bibliophile. He formed a library in Aelia Capitolina which contained the correspondence of the leading Christians of the time and was of great use to Eusebius when, a century later, he began to write his *Ecclesiastical History.*[1]

Origen, the friend of Alexander, followed him to the Holy Land in A.D. 216, the first of several visits. In A.D. 238 he settled at Caesarea, that beautiful city by the sea (now an almost equally beautiful ruin) and the earliest home of Gentile Christianity.[2] Origen knew the Holy Land well and approached it in much the same spirit as any modern scholar. He stated that he had been "on a search after the footsteps of Jesus and his disciples," and ventured the first known textual criticism based on local knowledge: the suggestion that the word "Bethany" in John 1:28 should read "Bethabara."

About the year A.D. 328 the Empress Helena, mother of Constantine the Great, made a pilgrimage to the Holy Land to pray for her family and also, it is said, to discover the scenes of our Lord's crucifixion and resurrection. She was nearly eighty years old at the time, though, said Eusebius, "full of youthful alacrity." Constantine had just built St. Peter's in Rome and had exposed the tomb of the Apostle to the veneration of the faithful. It was now his desire to reveal the Sepulchre of our Lord. Without hesitation, the Bishop of Jerusalem, Macarius, ordered the demolition of the temple of Venus, and, when the tons of rubble and rubbish had been removed, the tomb of Joseph of Arimathea, in which the body of Christ had been laid, was discovered, together with Calvary and, said later accounts, the True Cross. Upon this site Constantine ordered the Church of the Holy Sepulchre to be built "worthy of the most marvelous place in the world." When St. Helena went to Bethlehem, she demolished the temple of Adonis and under it was found the Grotto of the Nativity. Here another splendid church arose.

Thus already in the first decades of the fourth century the two chief pilgrimage shrines were established, and it was not long before pilgrims from distant parts of the Empire were setting out to offer up their devotions at these holy places. The first to leave a record of his journey was a man known as the Pilgrim of Bordeaux. Leaving his home in France in the year A.D. 333 (Constantine the Great was still alive), the traveler crossed the Alps and Northern Italy to Constantinople, then followed the excellent Byzantine trade and post roads across Asia Minor to Antioch—the route subsequently taken by the first Crusaders—and then went southward along the coast to Palestine.

Though Jerusalem, or Aelia Capitolina, was the goal of his journey, he turned aside before he had arrived there to visit other places; and these are most interesting as indications of the sites shown in those remote times to someone interested in the Bible. He visited Mount Gerizim, on which at that time was a temple of Jupiter, erected by Hadrian, and approached by a stairway of many hundreds of steps; at Nablus he saw Jacob's Well, which he did not associate, as the modern pilgrim does, with Jesus and the Woman of Samaria; he went on to Bethel with its Old Testament memories of Jacob's Vision, also with Jeroboam and the prophet who was killed by a lion.[3] The extraordinary thing is that though he was only a day's march from Nazareth and Galilee, he visited neither.

Arriving at last in Jerusalem, he saw the Church of the Holy Sepulchre three years before it was consecrated. What would one not give for a good description of the marvelous things he saw? But the Bordeaux Pilgrim was one of the worst of reporters, and this is all he could find to say about it:

"On the left hand is the little hill of Golgotha where the Lord was crucified. About a stone's throw from thence is a vault wherein His body was laid, and rose again on the third day. There, at present, by the command of the Emperor Constantine, has been built a basilica, that is to say, a church of wondrous beauty . . ."[4]

Again his omission is remarkable. Did he see the Cross discovered a few years earlier by St. Helena? His failure to mention this has led some learned men to suggest that it may not have been there and that the whole story of the discovery is a pious fabrication of later days. But it should be remembered that the Bordeaux Pilgrim possessed all the irritating deficiencies of a bad correspondent. We are all familiar with the person who has been present at some remarkable event, yet writes home about entirely trivial matters, or about himself. It may be that scholars place too much importance upon the evidential value of silence, which may indicate merely that the writer was a bad observer. Also, some people, when most impressed, are reduced to silence. The Pilgrim of Bordeaux seems to have been one of these.

He saw the site of the Jewish Temple, then occupied by Hadrian's temple to Jupiter and the statue of the Emperor, which was still there when St. Jerome went to live in Palestine. He went to the Mount of

Olives and mentions that vines were growing in the Garden of Gethsemane; he visited the church built over the grotto where Christ taught His disciples; and he saw the "little hill" of the Ascension before it had been built on. He went to Bethany to see the tomb of Lazarus, and to Jericho, to the Place of Baptism on the Jordan; and, like any modern pilgrim, he saw the Sycamore of Zacchaeus. He went to Bethlehem, visiting the Old Testament sites on the way, but saying of the Church of the Nativity merely that "a basilica has been built there by the orders of Constantine." He continued to Hebron, then began his long homeward journey.

What is surprising is that at this early date the main road of pilgrimage had been already mapped. It should be remembered that this pilgrim was traveling only nineteen years after the Edict of Milan, when Christianity had been proclaimed a tolerated religion; that the pagan temples were still open everywhere; that the Moslem did not exist (Mahomet was not born until some two hundred and thirty years later). Yet, in that remote world, the Pilgrim of Bordeaux had only to ask to be shown all the chief holy places which had remained sanctified and located in the long corporate memory of the Church.

In the fifty years which elapsed between the pilgrimage of the man from Bordeaux and the arrival in the Holy Land of St. Jerome's rich and fashionable friend, Paula, an enormous change occurred. Instead of the solitary inquisitive figure of the wanderer from Bordeaux, one now has an impression of large crowds from all parts of the Roman Empire traveling to Egypt to see the first cenobites of the Nitrian desert, then going on to Palestine to pray at the tomb of Christ. Paula was therefore in the fashion when she took ship from Ostia with her daughter, Eustochium, in A.D. 382. She was a fabulously rich woman who owned, among other properties, the entire town of Nicopolis, or Actium. Like many other wealthy and fashionable Roman matrons, she had become a convert and had given away immense sums in charity.

Paula met St. Jerome in Antioch and under his guidance the two women saw Jerusalem and the Holy Sepulchre and the Cenacle; Bethlehem and the Grotto of the Nativity; Nazareth; Cana of Galilee;

the Lake of Galilee and Capharnaum; in other words, exactly the same places seen today. Paula found herself so drawn to the Holy Land that she spent her life and her fortune there, founding in the course of the next twenty years numerous monasteries and hospices in Bethlehem, under the supervision of St. Jerome. Her pious life there, and the manner of her death, are described in the long letter which St. Jerome wrote to Eustochium to console her for the loss of her mother.[5]

From other letters we have an impression that in the time of St. Jerome the Holy Land was more crowded with pilgrims than at any other period until the Middle Ages. "Men rush here from all quarters of the world," he wrote, "the city is filled with people of every race and so great is the throng of men and women that here you would have to tolerate in its full dimensions an evil from which you desired to flee . . ."

From this point the literature of pilgrimage begins; and what a fascination there is in reading the accounts of those who were privileged to see the holy places before the rise of Islam, and who prayed in Constantine's great church when it was newly built. St. Silvia of Aquitania was the first pilgrim to describe the Easter Week ceremonies as she saw them in A.D. 385. She described the solemn services in the great basilica, a building which led into a superb atrium open to the sky, where the Rock of Calvary was exposed, thence into the beautiful rotunda which enshrined the tomb of Christ.

She revered the relics of the True Cross, which she described as being kept in a silver-gilt casket and removed on Good Friday to be revered on Calvary. The bishop and the deacons stood around it, as the people advanced to touch it with their lips, to prevent anyone from repeating the act of one who, some years before, under pretense of kissing the relic, had sunk his teeth in it and stolen a portion.

About this period a new type of pilgrim is to be noted: the uncritical venerator of relics. This tendency to stimulate religious emotion, which merged into commercialism, was just beginning in the time of St. Silvia, and was well established by A.D. 530, when the anonymous author of the *Breviarius de Hierosolyma*[6] was shown the emblems of the Crucifixion: the spear, the reed, the sponge, the crown of thorns, the rod of the scourging, the charger on which St. John's head had been carried, the stone which slew St. Stephen, and even the lamp by the light of which Jesus had taught His disciples.

Another pilgrim of the time, Theodosius, when visiting the Church of St. Mary in the Valley of Jehosaphat, was shown the couches upon which Jesus and the disciples had reclined during the Last Supper; and he gives the curious information that it was the custom for pilgrims to bring vegetarian meals to be eaten while they occupied these couches. In A.D. 570 Antoninus Martyr, when visiting the synagogue at Nazareth, was shown the schoolbook from which Jesus learnt the alphabet, and the school bench occupied by him.

So began a desire to minister to simple, or credulous, states of mind, which reached fantastic proportions during the Middle Ages. It is easy to be scornful about this aspect of pilgrimage, but more charitable to try and project oneself into a world where the devotion of simple folk needed such crutches and derived comfort from them.

The first of the many disasters which overwhelmed the holy places took place in A.D. 614, when the Persian army of Chosroes conquered Jerusalem, and, having sacked and demolished the churches, bore away the Cross itself into Persia. Hardly had the churches been rebuilt than, in A.D. 638, the city was seized by the army of the Caliph Omar, and so began that long Moslem occupation which has lasted until today, with only two brief intervals. These were eighty-eight years (1099-1187) during the Crusades, when the Latin Kingdom of Jerusalem was established, and thirty-one years (1917-1948) after the first World War, when Britain governed Palestine under a mandate from the League of Nations. This rule ended with the proclamation of the Jewish State of Israel on May 14, 1948.

The next day Israel was attacked on all her frontiers by Arab forces which assailed her from Syria and Lebanon on the north, from Iraq and Transjordan on the east, and from Egypt on the south. After more than six months of bitter fighting, four armistice agreements were arranged under the auspices of the United Nations in January, 1949, but, so far, not one of these has crystallized into peace. The frontier between the Jews and the Arabs remains frozen as it was at the time of the cease fire. The result of the new frontier between the Arab states and Israel is that the holy places are now split up between Jordan and Israel, and pilgrimage has consequently become more difficult and complicated than for centuries.

The whole of the old walled city of Jerusalem, with the Holy Sepulchre, the Mount of Olives, the Garden of Gethsemane, Bethlehem, with the Church of the Nativity, Jericho and the Jordan, and Bethany, are in Arab territory; while the Cenacle (the House of the Last Supper), Naim, Nazareth, the Lake of Galilee and Mount Tabor, are in Israel. No normal contact whatsoever exists between the two states. Jordan has never admitted the legal existence of Israel. A letter cannot be posted or a telephone call made from Jordan to Israel or from Israel to Jordan, and once the pilgrim has crossed the frontier from Jordan to Israel (except on the occasions of Christmas and Easter), he is not permitted to return unless he is given special privileges usually reserved for diplomats.

Everywhere the pilgrim goes on either side of the line he meets those heroes and guardians of the Holy Land, the Franciscans. The first Provincial was appointed in 1218, and as long as the Crusaders had a footing in the east, the fate of the Franciscans was bound up with theirs. "When at last the Latin Kings furled the flag beneath the walls of Acre in 1291 their flag (the fivefold cross) was handed over to the Franciscans who till this day fly it as a neutral international flag."[7]

For seven centuries their mission has been to guard and redeem the holy places and to help and succor the pilgrim. Often in difficulties with dissident Christians, Moslems and Jews, sometimes persecuted, the sons of St. Francis have led a crusade not of the sword but of the spirit. It is appropriate that the great French historian of the Crusades, Joseph Michaud, should have thanked them "in the name of all humanity." And, in the words of the Franciscan pamphlet just quoted: "This struggle has been one of the glories of the Franciscan Order. It has not been without its triumph. The dream of St. Francis has come true; his sons are still on guard by the Cradle and by the Tomb."

2

THE COMING

Nazareth

ONE AFTERNOON, as we came along a dusty road, we saw Nazareth lying before us upon the slope of a valley, and surrounded by an amphitheater of hills. The square white houses stood close together, amid vineyards and olive trees, and upon a distant ridge we saw a congregation of cypresses which everywhere in the Holy Land mark the footsteps of St. Francis. From a distance, Nazareth is seen wearing the shining mantle of love and affection with which the Christian centuries have clothed it; nearer, this magic disintegrates into a crowded Arab world of small shopkeepers, boys mounted upon the hindquarters of donkeys, and a steep main street, with a central drain or gulley, which descends to Mary's Well.

If there is one spot in the Holy Land where one can be confident that the Blessed Virgin stood with her infant Son, it is at this unchanging spring at Nazareth, whose waters have been drawn by women since life was first lived there. From a hill called Jebel es-Sîkh, one looks from a height of some sixteen hundred feet upon a map of the Old Testament. Three of the most famous mountains in the Holy Land are to be seen: Hermon to the north; Carmel to the west, washed by the Mediterranean waves; and, near at hand, Tabor to the east. Southward lies the plowland of the great Plain of Esdraelon, or Jezreel, hedgeless and treeless, so intensively cultivated by the modern Jews that it resembles a Canadian prairie. Upon that wide plain Gideon triumphed and Saul and Jonathan were overthrown; the abrupt mound that rises from the flat land is Megiddo, which holds the dusty ruins of Solomon's stables.

I THE ANNUNCIATION

UPON A platform of white rock, in Nazareth, is the sacred grotto which tradition claims to be the place of the Annunciation. In the course of the last thirteen centuries three churches have occupied the site, and a fourth, the largest of all, is about to replace the Franciscan basilica of 1730. As we walked up the steep slope to the monastery, we saw masons, with white dust in their hair, chipping away at the stone for the new church; and, as we glanced into the foundations for the new building, we saw traces of the Byzantine church of A.D. 600, and also of the church with which the Crusaders replaced it. Against the walls of the monastery were stacked Byzantine columns and Crusading capitals found in the excavations, some of which will perhaps be incorporated in the fourth Basilica of the Annunciation.

One approaches the Grotto of the Annunciation with memories of some of the most exquisite pictures in the world. No words have been more lovingly illustrated than those with which St. Luke describes the descent of the Angel Gabriel to announce her destiny to our Lady: "Hail, thou who art full of grace; the Lord is with thee; blessed art thou among women." One remembers a hundred pictures: the Angel alighting before a portico, or in a quiet garden where the Virgin sits with downcast eyes, or with hands raised in bewilderment ("She was much perplexed . . ."), while in the background a few cypress trees grow and a road winds into the hills, just as in Nazareth today.

One remembers elaborate Annunciations like that by Crivelli, in the National Gallery, London, where the Virgin is kneeling at a faldstool in surroundings of the utmost luxury and magnificence; or lovingly simple ones like that of Fra Angelico in the Convent of San Marco, in Florence, where the Angel has just risen from his knees and the Virgin sits on a rough wooden stool; or perhaps most graceful of all, Leonardo da Vinci's beautiful picture in the Uffizi, in which Gabriel has just alighted softly upon grass and flowers and the Virgin is seated at a small hand-loom, a reference to the ancient tradition that at the time she was weaving or spinning purple thread.

Several steps lead downward to the Grotto which, though now covered with marble, is in size, shape and origin essentially the same as many of the ancient and still inhabited houses of Nazareth, which are cut into the hillside and extended by building forward with stones or wood. The house was small and humble, and bore no relation to the spacious palaces and porticoes in which many great artists have placed the Annunciation. The crypt is no larger than a small room; and immediately above it will be erected the high altar of the new church. There is no site more sacred than this in the Holy Land, for, in the words beneath the altar, "*Verbum Caro Hic Factum Est*" ("Here the Word was made Flesh").

No pilgrim has left a record of the Byzantine church, and the first mention of the second church is that of a Russian abbot named Daniel, who made a pilgrimage in 1106, during the Crusades. The country round Nazareth was then so dangerous, and so full of "impious Saracens," that pilgrims were obliged to travel together with an armed escort. When he arrived at the church, the abbot found that "the Franks" had restored it beautifully, and he was hospitably entertained by a Latin bishop who was living in the monastery.

The most interesting of all pilgrims was St. Francis himself, who landed at Acre in 1219, on his way to preach the Gospel to the Sultan of Egypt. Naturally he visited Nazareth on his way south, "whither he was drawn," says his biographer, "by the sanctuary of the mystery of the Incarnation of the Word."[1] And today, as his brown-habited friars explain the history of their church, one remembers that it is due to their heroism and their devotion, and to their tenacity in the face of persecution, that the Grotto of the Annunciation is still a Christian shrine.

It is impossible to leave it without recalling that the most perfect of all medieval kings, St. Louis of France, went there with his queen,

Margaret, in 1254, after their release from four years of captivity in Egypt. His confessor[2] described the scene:

"The eve of the Annunciation of our Lady, after sleeping at Sepphoris, he put on a hair shirt and went to Cana of Galilee, then to Mount Tabor and arrived the same day at Nazareth. As soon as he came within sight of the holy town, he left the saddle and threw himself on both knees in prayer. Then proceeding on foot in all humility, he came to the holy town and entered the holy place of the Incarnation.

"That day he fasted on bread and water, in spite of his fatigue. With what devotion he behaved, with what solemnity and splendor he caused Vespers, Matins, Mass and other offices suited to such a feast to be celebrated is attested by several witnesses. More than one will announce and maintain that since the day when the Son of God took flesh of the Virgin Mary in this place, never was office celebrated with so much solemnity and devotion. The pious king, after assisting at Mass, said at the altar of the Annunciation, received Holy Communion. Lord Odo of Tusculum, Legate of the Holy See, celebrated Mass and preached a devout sermon."

Thirty-seven years later, when the Crusaders left the Holy Land and handed the flag of the Latin Kingdom to the Franciscans, the long battle for the holy places began. Franciscans were repeatedly killed or driven from their sanctuaries; but there were always more Franciscans. A pilgrim who ventured into Nazareth in 1449 found only one priest and two Christians, secretly dwelling "in the chapel where the angel saluted Mary"; in 1644, a French traveler spoke of three poor Christians in Nazareth, persecuted by the Turks. It was not until 1730 that the Franciscans were able to re-build their glorious church.

Opposite the monastery the friars have made a little garden which is well protected from the boys of Nazareth. The gate is kept locked. The only flower in bloom when we were there was, appropriately, the Mary-gold, which Shakespeare called, so charmingly, the "Mary-bud." There could hardly be a better place than a garden in Nazareth to reflect upon the beauty and the variety of the bouquet which the piety and the affection of gardeners, and of countryfolk generally, have dedicated to the Virgin. There are, of course, Rosemary, the Madonna Lily, the Pink Armeria ("Our Lady's Cushion"), the Campanula (her "looking-glass"), the Harebell (her "thimble"), and Our Lady's Smock, mentioned by Shakespeare,

When daisies pied and violets blue
And lady's smock all silver white,
And cuckoo buds of yellow hue
Do paint the meadows with delight.

In France foxgloves are sometimes called *gants de Notre Dame;* in England the Canterbury Bell was once named "Our Lady's Glove"; the Fuschia is "Our Lady's Ear-drops"; the Black Briony, "Our Lady's Seal"; the Adiantum, or Maidenhair Fern, "Our Lady's Hair." No doubt one could greatly increase in beauty and size this loving nosegay.

We said good-by to the Franciscans and went down into the white town.

II THE VISITATION

FIVE MILES to the southwest of Jerusalem, the road, winding through the stony Judaean Hills, passes into a valley whose slopes are dotted with box-like houses rising from terraced gardens and vineyards. This is Ain Karem, or Ein Karim, the traditional birthplace of the Baptist. Upon one side of the valley stands the Church of St. John; facing it, upon the other side, is the Church of the Visitation. Both these sites have been visited by pilgrims since the third and fourth centuries.

After the Annunciation, the Virgin traveled "in all haste" to this village at the behest of the Angel. "See moreover," he said, "how it fares with your cousin Elizabeth; she is old, yet she, too, has conceived a son; she who was reproached with barrenness is now in her sixth month, to prove that nothing can be impossible with God."[3] In Ain Karem, Mary greeted her elderly cousin, and then spoke the *Magnificat,* words which have rung in splendor down the centuries.

The Church of St. John lies against the hillside and bears traces of many periods, and also of its tragic history. An old mosaic pavement inside the porch shows peacocks, doves, partridges, flowers and fruit, and bears the words in Greek, "Hail, Martyrs of God," a reference to the destruction of the church by the Samaritans in the sixth century and the massacre of all the monks. The site then lay in ruins until the Crusades; afterwards it became a mosque. In 1485 the Friars Minor managed to obtain possession of the Grotto, but were unable to restore the church or to settle there in security until the seventeenth century.

The church is now served by Spanish Franciscans, and we were greeted by Father Jesus from Valencia, who, like so many Spaniards, bears the Redeemer's name. The church is Spanish in appearance, with beautiful glazed tiles and fine iron-work. A few steps lead down to the Grotto of the Nativity of St. John, entirely encased in marble, where a star, or rather, perhaps, tongues of fire, bear the words, *"Hic Praecursor Domini Natus Est."* Upon this site the *Benedictus* sounded for the first time.

We crossed the valley to the opposite slope, where the Church of the Visitation forms a remarkable contrast to that of St. John. Here is a perfect example of the type of shrine which the devout Italian architect, Antonio Barluzzi, has been erecting in the Holy Land for the past thirty years. He has covered the land with a number of beautiful churches, as striking as they are unusual. They are a threefold tribute:

Birthplace of John the Baptist, Ain Karem

Church of the Visitatio
Ain Kare

Well, Grotto of Visitation, Church of the Visitation, Ain Karem

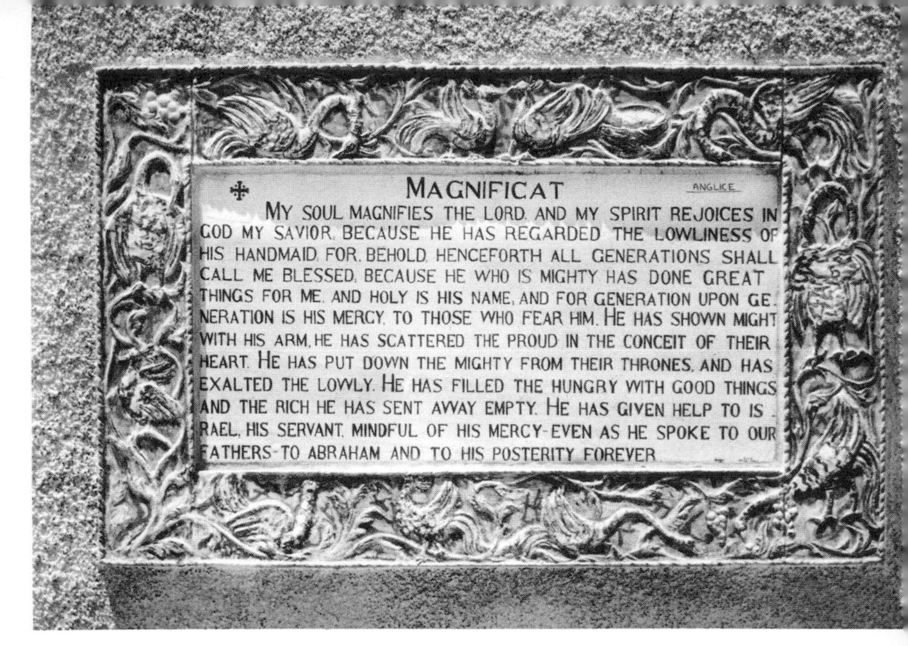

One of a series of tablets with the *Magnificat* in almost every language, Church of the Visitation, Ain Karem

to the holy places; to his own devotion to them; and to the Franciscan Order which gave him so free a hand.

This church is as Italian as the one opposite is Spanish. A decorative iron screen of great beauty leads into a courtyard in which stand the church and its campanile. High on the west wall, beneath an entrance portico, is a beautiful mosaic large enough to be seen across the valley, a work designed by Biagetti in the Vatican Mosaic Studios. It represents in delicate colors our Lady, clothed in white, seated upon an ass as she is guided by angels to Ain Karem. This is one of the most striking modern mosaics in the Holy Land.

Inside, one steps into Italy: Giotto-like frescoes cover the walls and the Florentine ceiling; the bronze doors, the chandeliers, and the altar furnishing are all unmistakably Italian. A flight of steps descends to a lower church in which there is an ancient spring whose water was drunk by most of the early pilgrims. On the boundary wall in the garden are set some forty porcelain plaques on which the *Magnificat* is inscribed in as many different languages.

One leaves this lovely church with the majestic canticle ringing in one's ears:

"My soul magnifies the Lord; my spirit has found joy in God, who is my Saviour, because he has looked graciously upon the lowliness of his handmaid. Behold, from this day forward all generations will call me blessed; because he who is mighty, he whose name is holy, has wrought for me his wonders. . . ."

III THE NATIVITY

BETHLEHEM is first seen through the branches of ancient olive trees which line the road. Flat-roofed houses, like a flock of white pigeons, are gathered upon a ridge and descend by terraces into a valley. The scene, entirely different from the harsh severity of Jerusalem, is softened by an air of tranquility and grace.

The town is inhabited by Moslems and Christian Arabs, mostly Latin or Eastern Rite Catholics, though there are also numerous Greek Orthodox, Armenians, Syrians and Copts. In a country where the villagers still wear their beautiful regional dress, the women of Bethlehem are distinguished by a headdress which some say is a relic of the Crusades and was copied from the steeple hat—the *hennin*—worn by the ladies of France who followed their lords to the Holy Land. Others

Bethlehem

"Angel of the Lord" above entrance, Chapel of the Angels and Shepherds, Shepherds' Field, near Bethlehem

think that the ladies may have taken the fashion to Europe from the East. The headdress is a small red fez sewn with coins and covered with a flowing white veil. When the women of Bethlehem attend some great ceremony in the Church of the Nativity, many a newcomer has imagined the church to be filled with nuns.

St. Jerome, who went to live at Bethlehem in 386, said that a thousand paces to the east of the town lay the field where the angels announced the birth of Christ to the shepherds.[4] That is just about the distance, over a rough and stony track, to the exquisite Canadian chapel of the Angels and the Shepherds. This little rotunda is like a Christmas carol. The light flows joyously through its windows, and one stands in it with the feeling that the perfect words of St. Luke have been interpreted in stone. It is the last work of Barluzzi, completed in 1954, just before age and disappointment drove him from the Holy Land. The Angel of the Lord is seen above the door descending to announce the news, and the altar is supported at the four corners

Chapel, Shepherds' Field, near Bethlehem

by the bronze figures of kneeling shepherds. In the course of centuries shrine has followed shrine upon this site, but none can have been more beautiful than the little sanctuary which now bears the maple leaf among its sculpture.

Edersheim,[5] writing with a profound knowledge of the Jewish background of the New Testament, has much to say of the significance of those particular shepherds and those particular flocks, but one thinks not of such learned works in that place, but rather of the earliest memories of childhood: of the first pictures remembered and loved; the dark night; the wondering shepherds shielding their eyes from the shining glory of the Angel; and the Angel bidding them not to be afraid, for "This day, in the city of David, a Saviour has been born for you, the Lord Christ himself."

One glances across the Shepherds' Field, now sown with wheat, towards the House of Bread, which is Bethlehem, where the terraced houses and the olive trees group themselves round the basilica which Constantine the Great erected seventeen centuries ago.

One enters the Church of the Nativity by way of an oblong opening in a blocked-up doorway so low that it is necessary to bend down, a precaution taken centuries ago to deter armed Moslems from riding into the church on horseback. Once inside, the sight of the venerable basilica, solemn and Roman, dark and dusky, and sunk in incredible antiquity, is one of the most satisfying in the Holy Land. What is not Constantinian in this church dates from the restoration under Justinian in 531; and it is the only building in the Holy Land of this size and importance to come down to us substantially unchanged.

In a long story of destruction and hate, it is good to know that at least one church in Palestine bore a charmed life. It is said that when the Persians, who burnt down the Church of the Holy Sepulchre, and other churches, in 614, came to Bethlehem, they spared the church because they saw with amazement an exterior mosaic (no longer there) which depicted the Magi in Persian dress.

When the Caliph Omar came to Bethlehem in 638, instead of demolishing the basilica, he entered to pray in the western apse, which conveniently faced Mecca; and for centuries Moslems continued to pray there, and even to make pilgrimages to Bethlehem. Though

Present entrance with two closed former entrances above, Basilica of Nativity, Bethlehem

the church has structurally remained as it was in Byzantine days, no trace of the splendor is left, no gold mosaics, no glass-like marble in which the early pilgrims said they could see their faces as in a mirror. All such gorgeousness has long since fallen a prey to the weather and marauding infidels.

Few people, however, spend much time in the splendid nave of the basilica, but pass immediately to the dark Grotto of the Nativity beneath the high altar. Here they see, by the light of many candles, a rocky cavern disguised by rich fabrics and tapestries where, upon a slab of marble, a fourteen-pointed star beneath the altar marks the traditional site of the Nativity. The inscription that surrounds it has been almost kissed away, *"Hic De Virgine Maria, Jesus Christus Natus Est."* Silver lamps hanging in a half circle above the Star of Bethlehem are shared by the three communities: Franciscans, Greeks and Ar-

Star of Bethlehem under the Altar of the Nativity,
Grotto of Nativity, Basilica, Bethlehem

Manger of Jesus, Grotto of Nativity, Basilica, Bethlehem

menians. Four steps go down to the small oratory of the Manger, where the Virgin placed her newborn Child; and it was here that the shepherds knelt to adore Him.

He came all so still
Where His mother was,
As dew in April
That falleth on the grass.

Mother and maiden
Was never none but she!
Well may such a lady
God's mother be.

IV THE FLIGHT INTO EGYPT

Bethlehem was the place where the caravans for Egypt were made up, and we learn from Jeremias that it was sometimes necessary to wait there for some time. "They went off and made their home for a time at Chamaan, near Bethlehem, thinking to take refuge in Egypt . . ."

Only one Evangelist, St. Matthew, mentions the Flight into Egypt, and there is nothing in his words to suggest that the Holy Family traveled, as ordinary people did, in the company of merchants and others on that long journey across the ancient trade route through Hebron and Beersheba to the Delta. "He rose up, therefore, while it was still night, and took the child and his mother with him, and withdrew into Egypt . . ."

Though the other three Gospels are silent about the Flight into Egypt, there is a wealth of descriptive detail in the apocryphal "infancy gospels," and most agree that the two places associated with the Holy Family were Heliopolis, which was the Greek name for the ancient Egyptian city of On, and Babylon, which was the ancient name for Cairo.

In the reign of Augustus, Egypt had a Jewish population which has been estimated at a hundred and twenty thousand, mostly concentrated in Alexandria, Babylon and Heliopolis;[6] and there can have been scarcely a family in Palestine in the time of Christ which did not have a relative or a friend in Egypt. Heliopolis is often mentioned in the Old Testament. The city is called Bêh Shemish by Jeremias, which means the "House of the Sun," a reference to the great temple of the Sun God, Rā, where the legends of the Phoenix originated. The priests of Rā were noted for their great learning.

"Flight into Egypt," Milk Grotto, Bethleh

"I went to Heliopolis," says Herodotus, "for the Heliopolitans are esteemed the most learned in history of all the Egyptians." Joseph was married to the daughter of Potiphare—Pa-ta-pa-Rā, the "Gift of Rā" —who was priest at Heliopolis, and many ancient writers say that Moses was born there and educated in the priestly university. Strabo is not alone in calling him "an Egyptian priest named Moses." In Heliopolis he "was well trained in all the learning of the Egyptians."[7]

Thus, in traveling to Egypt, the Holy Family would be joining the largest Jewish colony in the world at that time, though Heliopolis in the age of Augustus was no longer the great religious center known to Joseph and to Moses. The priests of On, finding the Hellenistic age incompatible with their traditions and beliefs, had long since deserted their sanctuaries; and it was to a declining, if not a ruined, city to which the Holy Family came, though many of the great temples and obelisks were still standing.

The obelisk in Central Park, New York, and "Cleopatra's Needle" on the Thames Embankment, London, were both erected originally at Heliopolis, and had been moved to Alexandria some twelve years before the birth of Christ. Both these monuments were set up in front of the temple of Rā by the Pharaoh Thuthmes III, about 1500 B.C., and some believe that the Exodus took place in the next reign. If so, those who heedlessly pass these monuments every day may reflect that it is highly probable that Moses saw them, and that they were already of enormous antiquity at the time of the Flight into Egypt.

The traveler who follows up the legends of the Flight will find himself in a dusty town called El Matarîya, which is now practically a suburb of Cairo. The countryside for six miles around was once scattered with the ruins of the great Heliopolis, but today the only remaining relic is a solitary granite obelisk standing in the middle of a field, the last memorial of a once great and powerful city. Any resident of Matarîya will lead the visitor to the Virgin's Tree, a vast old sycomore propped up with pieces of timber and surrounded by a wall.

The legend is that as the Holy Family rested in the shade of this tree the Virgin washed her Son's clothes in a nearby well, and balsam trees sprang up wherever the drops of water fell. There are no balsam trees now and this story is a confused memory of the balsam gardens

Legendary resting place of the Holy Family, Matarîya, near Cairo

which once stood there, possibly grown from cuttings from the famous groves at Jericho at the command of Cleopatra. The celebrated "Garden of Balm," or "Garden of Herbs," visited by medieval pilgrims, has now shrunk to a squalid and miserable enclosure where the dead old sycomore looks older than any tree in the world. Actually, it was planted as recently as 1672, probably from a seed or cutting of another sycomore which had been standing there for centuries.

Though the tree may be dead, its potency as a worker of miracles is not, as we were soon to learn. A local man, a Copt, told us that when a housing project that looms over the tree was erected recently, orders were given to cut down the sycomore and a man was actually found willing to commit this act. Before he could do so, however, while indeed his ax was poised, his arm became paralyzed. In proof of this the man took us round to the back of the "garden" and showed us that the two wings of the building were of unequal length because, after this incident, the builders were forced to halt their construction at a respectful distance from the Virgin's Tree.

The *sycomore* of the Bible bears no resemblance to the *sycamore* of North America. It is a huge shade tree that bears what resemble small figs, which are eaten by the Egyptians. They pluck them when almost ripe and prick them with a pin which they say is necessary if the "figs" are to be eatable. It is also a different tree from the *sycamine* tree, mentioned in the Gospels, which is the black mulberry. It is time, however, that the old sycomore of Matarîya should be decently interred and another planted in its place. Perhaps the French Jesuits, who have a church a few yards away, will do so. Above the porch of their church are the words, "*Sanctae Familiae in Aegypto Exuli,*" and this must be one of the few churches that commemorate the Flight into Egypt. The walls are decorated with attractive frescoes which show the Holy Family in flight and entering Heliopolis, when, according to the Coptic legend, an earthquake occurred which sent all the idols crashing from their pedestals.

The only site in Cairo linked with the Flight into Egypt is the crypt of the Coptic church of St. Sergius, or Abu Sarga, in the depths of the Old City. Like all Coptic churches, Abu Sarga appears to have been standing since the beginning of time, and it may well be that the crypt dates from the first century. The priest led the way and pointed out to us a little shelf, or alcove, which is the traditional spot where the Virgin is said to have cradled the infant Jesus. Pilgrims have been visiting this crypt since the early Middle Ages, and they still do so.

3

THE MINISTRY

I BAPTISM

THOSE WHO have explored the byways of Nazareth will have noticed the number of carpenters' shops to be found there. Several streets smell of pine shavings and through open doors one may see Arab carpenters making furniture and a variety of agricultural implements.

"Is not this the carpenter," is the only hint in the Gospels that during the hidden years, when Jesus "advanced in wisdom with the years, and in favour both with God and with men," He assisted St. Joseph and worked as a carpenter Himself. Many attempts have been made to find allusions to this occupation in the parables and sayings of Christ, but with little success, unless "Cleave the wood and there you shall find me," in the *Sayings of Jesus*, can be accepted as such.

One recalls a striking picture by Holman Hunt of an imaginary moment at this period in the life of Christ. It is called *The Shadow of Death* (not perhaps the perfect title) and is to be seen in the Art Gallery in Manchester, England. It shows our Lord as a young carpenter who has put aside His hammer and nails and, tired by the day's work, stretches His arms wearily, casting upon the wall the shadow of a cross, a sight observed by His mother. It is an arresting picture and, like so much of Holman Hunt's work in the Holy Land, the result of long meditation.

Synagogue where Jesus preached, Nazareth

"St. Joseph died during this time," says Ronald Cox. "Jesus then worked to support himself and his mother. All his human characteristics came from her; not only his physical appearance, but his manner of speech; the graciousness and tenderness which he shows in later life came from daily intimate life with his mother. The rest of us receive much from both father and mother; this child alone of all mankind was the son of his mother."[1]

This mysterious period ended when "Jesus himself had now reached the age of about thirty"[2] and "came from Galilee and stood before John at the Jordan, to be baptised by him."[3]

Since the time of the Pilgrim of Bordeaux the traditional place of the Baptism has been a stretch of the river about five miles from the northern end of the Dead Sea. One descends from the comparative coolness of Jerusalem into a trench of heat as the desolate road loops and spirals down past Bethany, past the Inn of the Good Samaritan, which is now an Arab police station. One can feel the heat becoming greater every moment, as one descends into the undulating desert where nothing moves save, maybe, a herd of camels driven by a few Bedouin.

At last the palm trees and the gardens of Jericho are seen: a tropical little town quivers in the heat and irrigation canals tinkle and ripple through its dense vegetation. The famous balsam groves which Antony gave to Cleopatra are no longer there; instead, there are groves which produce all the bananas sold in Jerusalem. Outside the town the land is covered with a spiky bush, *Zizyphus spina Christi,* from which it is believed the crown of thorns was made. Still the road descends beyond Jericho, to end at a ford called by the Arabs *Makkâdet el Hajlâ,* the "bathing place of the pilgrims," more than a thousand feet below the level of the sea. "There may be something on the surface of another planet to match the Jordan Valley: there is nothing on this," wrote George Adam Smith.

A small blue stream flows southward to the Dead Sea between steep banks bordered with willows, acacia, tamarisks, and the Reed of Jordan—*Agnus castus*—which is a kind of flowering bamboo. The Jordan here cannot be more than forty feet wide; anyone could toss a stone across it, and one looks at it amazed to think that it is the most important river in the world. Hymns, spirituals, references to Jordan's "waves," or to Jordan "rolling," prepare one for a spectacular river; and many are the pilgrims who have been disappointed. The physical dimensions of the Jordan are a lesson in values.

This is perhaps the first holy site which appeals to the heart rather than to the intelligence or the understanding: nothing here requires elucidation or explanation. In this quiet spot, where the birds sing among the reeds and the gardens, is the place where Jesus was baptized. Yet is it quite as simple?

"The baptism of Jordan was a prelude to the baptism of which He would later speak, the baptism of His Passion. Twice afterwards did He refer to His baptism. The first time was when James and John asked Him if they could sit on either side of Him in His Kingdom. In answer, He asked them if they were ready to be baptised with the baptism which He was going to receive. Thus His baptism of water looked forward to His baptism of blood. The Jordan flowed into the red rivers of Calvary."[4]

In the days when Russia was "holy Russia," it was the custom for crowds of pilgrims, wearing the cheap printed cotton shrouds still sold in Jerusalem, to bathe in the Jordan; and this custom is of great antiquity. The pilgrim Theodoric wrote in 1172:

"When our humble selves had also visited this place in order to pray there, desiring to wash in the waters of the Jordan with the rest, we descended the mountain after sunset, just as darkness was coming on; and looking out from its heights over the flat plain below us, we saw, according to our reckoning, more than sixty thousand men standing thereon, almost all of them carrying candles in their hands—all of whom could be seen by the infidels from the mountains of Arabia beyond Jordan."[5]

We gazed from the pleasant green gardens of the west bank across the little river to the desolate wilderness that rolled formlessly towards the mountains of Moab. One thought of locusts; but there could be little honey in such a spot. It was one of those days when the light penetrated the slightest crack or crevice. The mountains were drawn

Site of Christ's Baptism,
River Jordan, near Jericho

nearer and we saw their flanks wrinkled by an eternity of rain and erosion delicately etched in thin lines of blue. One reads of the "music of the spheres"; there is also a music of desert places, a music composed of absolute silence and stillness. But that is an entirely modern conception of the desert. None of the ancient hermits and anchorites would have recognized it: they went into the desert not to escape temptation but to invite it, and to pit their spiritual strength against the wiles of the devil who, in their belief, inhabited these wastes. Upon the heights of the distant mountains above the Dead Sea, Moses looked down upon the Promised Land, and, in Herod's great stronghold of Machaerus, the Baptist was slain.

We stood on the edge of the Dead Sea where an hotel, Arab-owned and managed by a Swiss, advertises itself rather ambiguously as "the lowest spot on earth." There were a couple of beach umbrellas and a suggestion that visitors had been bathing. There was no other evidence of life. Though fish carried by the Jordan into the Dead Sea expire in a manner of minutes, the waters look anything but dead when the sun gives them a sparkle and the blue waves curl over on the beach. To dip a finger into the Dead Sea and to touch one's lips is to taste some nauseating medicine, and five minutes after the finger is white with encrusted chemicals.

The golden, impenetrable mountains rise above the western shores like slag heaps from some colossal furnace. If man ever lands upon the Moon, this must be the kind of landscape he will see. Somewhere, tilted upon a plateau within sight of the Dead Sea, are the ruins of the Qumran monastery where the Dead Sea Scrolls were written centuries before Christ, and hidden, no one knows why, in caves, packed in tall jars according to the Biblical precept: "Take these two pieces of writing, the sealed deed within, and the covering of it that is open to view, and keep them in some jar of clay, where they can remain long without damage."[6]

Somewhere in those forbidding mountains is the small cave where a Bedouin goatherd, seeking a lost kid, found the first of the scrolls in 1947. History does not relate whether he discovered the animal, but he discovered the richest find of its kind ever made, and one that will occupy scholars for generations to come. Since the first discovery, it is said that something like $150,000 has passed into the eager hands of the Bedouin, and the mountains have become a kind of desert Klondike. There is still some furtive dealing in Bethlehem, which is the headquarters of the scroll market. The current price is $18 a square inch. Unfortunately the setting of a measurement of this kind has had the result that manuscripts are being broken down into inch squares, thus giving those who already have a lifetime of work before them, a good deal of unnecessary trouble.

Jerusalem has always been a place of puzzles and mysteries, and none more puzzling than the jigsaw of the Dead Sea Scrolls now to be seen in a long room in the Palestine Archaeological Museum. They call it the "Scrollery." Sandwiched between sheets of plate-glass are thousands of parchment fragments, few larger than an inch or two square, which archaeologists are painfully and brilliantly piecing together.

On the Israeli side, Dr. Yigael Yadin, who was once a general in

Mount of Temptation, near Jericho

Dead Sea Scrolls, Hebrew University, Jerusalem

his country's army, showed us the four complete Dead Sea Scrolls acquired for Israel at a cost of $250,000 and now splendidly housed at the new Hebrew University. They had been hawked round America for years by a Syrian cleric who had failed to find any buyers when, by an extraordinary coincidence, Dr. Yadin, on a lecture tour of the United States in 1953, hit their trail and managed to buy them. They were in a black trunk in the storage vaults of the Waldorf-Astoria Hotel in New York and had been advertised in a small notice in the Wall Street Journal!

II SAMARIA

FROM JERUSALEM to a few miles south of Nazareth the frontier of Jordan forms a great bulge towards the sea, leaving Israel with a forty-mile-long strip of coast land in places only about fourteen miles wide. Arab sentries sit on the hills, gazing straight across Israel to the shipping on the Mediterranean. The bulge represents the greatest Arab advance towards the sea at the time of the cease fire in 1949. It means that Samaria is in Jordan, and also, as the frontier runs north of Nablus, no one can take the direct short cut through Samaria to Nazareth. To do so, it is necessary to return to Jerusalem and cross into Israel, a detour of some three hundred miles!

The northern road, though now a cul-de-sac, is well worth traveling, for it leads to Jacob's Well, at Sichar. In a land where great agricultural changes have occurred in the past thirty years, this countryside is perhaps the finest surviving stretch of old Palestine. In Israel the tractor, irrigation and scientific agriculture have transformed a once barren land into a fruitful country, and even the stones have miraculously disappeared. But ancient habits and customs have also vanished, and only in Jordan may one still see the Biblical life of other days preserved by the conservatism of the Canaanite peasant, who is the Arab.

It was a beautiful morning in late spring when we set out for Samaria. The clouds hung above stony hills which were stained red and blue with the last of the anemones—the "lilies of the field"—and upon each side of the road, and in the valleys, peasants were plowing the earth and sowing summer crops. We saw men turning the rich-looking, coffee-colored soil with wooden plows of a pattern to be seen on the tomb paintings of ancient Egypt; sometimes a small strip of good

earth between stony ground was being cultivated in order to grow a few square yards of wheat or barley. Barefoot women in red skirts moved across the land, carrying upon their heads great loads of fodder, or thorns to crackle underneath their pots, and disappeared gracefully among the rocks to some white village; sleek cranes stalked over the fields or stood, delicately and reflectively, gazing down into the growing crops; and here and there a shepherd led his sheep, staff in hand, not following them, as shepherds do in Europe.

We came to a man who might have been the sower who went forth to sow. We asked if it would be possible to take a photograph. The man, though courteous, said no. He had cousins in the United States who would be ashamed to see him dressed as a peasant and wearing a *kaffiyeh*. To this, there was no answer, so, exchanging compliments, we parted. In a mile or so we saw a young girl, her outer garment rolled round her waist, exposing a pair of red spotted Turkish trousers, walking slowly behind a plow as she directed seed into the furrows from a tin funnel. The plowman, his plow drawn by an ox and a mule "unevenly yoked," in the words of St. Paul, proved to have no relatives in the United States, and was not only pleased to be photographed but also anxious to show our boys how to turn a furrow! So we traveled north into Samaria, thinking that, in the tranquility of this frugal land, the hills and the valleys rejoiced in the ministrations of its children.

When we arrived at Sichar, we saw a rocky landscape and two motor coaches precariously perched upon a slope near the gate of a Greek monastery. We descended to the ruins of an impressive Crusading church which had been erected to enshrine Jacob's Well where Jesus met the Woman of Samaria. Now a small Greek chapel covers the well, which is some distance below the present level of the earth.

Seated amongst the ruins were the pilgrims who had come in the two coaches. There were a number of aged women dressed in black, and so alike in appearance that they might have been members of the same family. Their heads were covered in shawls and each one grasped a small bag in which were her possessions. They were part of a pilgrimage from the Greek isle of Patmos, where, beside "the sea and the mighty things," St. John is said to have written the Apocalypse.

Unequally yoked," Samaria

Led by two Greek priests, venerable and vastly bearded, they had arrived by ship at Jaffa, as the Russian pilgrims used to do. They had the faith which moves mountains and were not burdened by the little flicker of learning which some of us carry about the Holy Land. Talking to them, as best one could, was like meeting contemporaries of Arculf or St. Willibald, or indeed any of the medieval pilgrims. Their faces were an inextricable network of lines and wrinkles, and in each face one seemed to read a record of more than half a century of toil, labor and patience, culminating in this great moment when they found themselves in the land of their Redeemer.

One of the old priests came up and said there was room for six more in the little chapel above the well: rising, and making the sign of the cross from right to left, as the Greeks do, these women of Patmos followed him down the dark steps to the scene immortalized by St. John.

The well at which Jesus met the Woman of Samaria was once in the open air and on ground level. Today the land has risen some twenty feet and the little chapel, in which the well is seen by candlelight, is splashed with water. It is surrounded by a wellhead from which it is possible to lower a bucket. We watched the old women of Patmos do so, and when it came up brimming with ice cold water, they drank it and, dipping their hands in it, wet their faces.

It is one of the unarguable sites. No other well for miles around answers the description. Here our Lord rested and discoursed with the woman on the living waters of life, and astounded her by His knowledge that she had had five husbands and was living in sin. This sinful woman was the first human being to whom Christ announced His divinity. "Jesus said to her, I who speak to thee, am the Christ."

"Two classes of people make up the world," writes Bishop Sheen, "those who have found God, and those who are looking for Him—thirsting, hungering, seeking! And the great sinners come closer to Him than the proud intellectuals! Pride swells and inflates the ego; gross sinners are depressed, deflated and empty. They, therefore, have room for God. God prefers a loving sinner to a loveless 'saint.' Love can be trained; pride cannot. The man who thinks that he knows will rarely find truth; the man who knows he is a miserable unhappy sinner, like

Jacob's Well, Samaria, near Nablus

the woman at the well, is closer to peace, joy and salvation than he knows."[7]

What comforting words!

The Latin Church has preserved no legends about the Woman of Samaria, but the Greek Church knows her as Photina and remembers her on March 20. A tradition as early as the sixth century says that she went to live in Carthage, where she had two sons; one became a Christian teacher and the other died for his faith. She herself is said to have died in prison.[8]

Samaritan high priest with
scrolls of the Law (Pentateuch),
Samaria

The last relics of the Samaritan sect are to be found in the shadow of Mount Gerizim, in the town of Nablus. There are about three hundred and forty of them, indistinguishable in appearance from Arabs and all inbred. The majority are small tradesmen and artisans, but the priesthood enjoys more leisure and spends a great deal of its time on the lookout for tourists. The synagogue is a bare, modern hall where a copy of the Pentateuch inscribed on parchment is to be seen mounted on heavy silver rollers.

The word "good," applied to the Samaritan in the parable, derived its point from the conviction in Gospel times that Samaritans did not come within this category. A constant stream of pilgrims and tourists descends today upon Nablus, anxious to romanticize the survivors of an ancient race, but many depart impressed by the commercialization of this remnant.

III GALILEE

NO ONE who has explored the lakeside of Galilee, or has taken a boat in the hush of morning, or during that enchanted hour at sunset when the opposite hills glow as pinkly as a sea-shell, will ever forget the serenity that lies upon this now almost deserted region. But it was not always so. In the time of Christ, Galilee was a busy, densely populated district humming with the activity of a ring of fishing towns and villages; the place, too, where Herod Antipas had built his new town named Tiberias in compliment to the reigning Caesar.

Josephus was probably exaggerating when he said that in his time Galilee contained two hundred and four towns and villages, with an average population of fifteen thousand, which would mean a total of three million people. At any rate, his figures indicate that Galilee impressed him as crowded. Upon the eastern mountains, across the lake, were the Greek-speaking cities of the Decapolis, whose ruined temples, theaters and baths at Jerash, Philadelphia, and Gadara astonish the traveler as an indication of the thriving Hellenistic life which existed there in the time of Christ. The stampede of the Gerasene swine is a lifelike touch, for no such animals would have been tolerated on the Jewish shores opposite. Galilee was therefore the meeting place of Jew and Gentile. The Galilean Jew was a tolerant person and, as such, suspected by the Scribes and Pharisees. He was also a provincial who spoke with an accent. It was St. Peter's Galilean accent which betrayed him to the servants of the high priest: "It is certain that thou art one of them; even thy speech betrays thee."[9]

The pilgrim who follows the footsteps of Jesus today must forget the abandoned lakeside as it is now, and imagine it crowded with human beings, and on one of the main roads of the world. I wrote the following some years ago on the significance of Galilee:

"By going into Galilee Jesus performed a symbolic act. He turned his back upon the world of the Old Testament, and from the moment of his turning away the New Testament begins.

"Everyone must feel how different are these two worlds. In the New Testament we seem to have emerged from a dark, fierce eastern world into a clear light that is almost European. In fact Rome is already in sight. The center of the Old Testament world is rigid, exclusive Jerusalem; the center of the New Testament world is international Galilee, a country crossed in the time of Christ by the great military roads from the north and by the caravan routes from the east, a country in which a man seen in the distance might be an imperial messenger riding to Caesarea with tidings of the Emperor's death, or a tax-gatherer from the main road to Damascus, or a Greek architect on his way to build a new theatre in Jerash in the Decapolis.

"This busy international corridor was the place in which Jesus taught. He alone of all the prophets who had come out of Israel deliberately cut Himself off from the spiritual stronghold of Judaea. And the roads He chose to tread were not the roads of the priests and the rabbis but the roads of the world. So in the road that runs over a hill from Nazareth to the Sea of Galilee a man detects the first promise of Christianity."[10]

Synagogue, Capharnaum

The Galilean Ministry was based at Capharnaum, "His own city,"[11] where Jesus lived and to which He returned at the conclusion of His journeys. In this beautiful and unique part of the world, six hundred and eighty feet below the sea, and in a humid, semi-tropical heat which in summer makes the early morning and the evening the most enjoyable times of the day, Jesus "went about all their cities and villages, teaching in their synagogues, preaching the gospel of the kingdom, and curing every kind of disease and infirmity,"[12] for a period which some scholars estimate as three years. Here He called the Apostles to be with Him and "to understand the secret of God's kingdom";[13] and in this beautiful land of low hills and blue water He roused the hatred of His enemies. The roadside of Galilee led onward to Calvary.

From the hill behind Tiberias one can see the whole sweep of the lake. Far to the north, escorted by clouds, Mount Hermon bears its snow-cap sometimes into summer; to the northwest is the little Plain of Gennesaret, the central point of the Galilean Ministry, where, amid trees and bushes which advance to the water's edge, are the sites of Magdala, Bethsaida and Capharnaum. Immediately below, the square white houses of Tiberias rise from the lakeside and straggle up the hill, and, to the south, the lake ends in a belt of woodland through which the Jordan flows on the first stage of its serpentine journey to the Dead Sea. An impressive feature, across the water, are the opposite shores—now Syrian territory—which change in color from brown to pink and from pink to mauve, and emerge sometimes with such clarity that every fissure is seen thinly penciled in shadow.

We explored the ruins of the synagogue at Capharnaum, which some believe is the actual building erected by the centurion,[14] and the most impressive ruin on the lakeside. If such indeed is its identity, it is one of the most precious of all relics from the time of Christ. It is a puzzling building. A classical screen of Corinthian columns, with its architrave, rises above a series of paved courtyards intersected by low walls upon which the Franciscans, who have excavated here, have placed a bewildering variety of carved stones and richly decorated capitals. Some bear emblems of flowers and trees; others depict a pomegranate, a palm tree, a bunch of grapes, even a bearded seahorse with a horn upon its forehead. Above the door was once a frieze of angels, but only the wings survive.

One thinks of the miracles performed here: the demoniac, the man with the withered hand, and, above all, one remembers that scene, with its underlying violence and doom, when Jesus said to a great mob, pressing round demanding more miracles, more loaves and more fishes:

"It is I who am the bread of life; he who comes to me will never be hungry, he who has faith in me will never know thirst. (But you, as I have told you, though you have seen me, do not believe in me.) . . . Your fathers, who ate manna in the desert, died none the less; the bread which comes down from heaven is such that he who eats of it never dies. I myself am the living bread that has come down from heaven. If anyone eats of this bread, he shall live for ever. . . . Believe me when I tell you this; you can have no life in yourselves, unless you eat the flesh of the Son of Man, and drink his blood. The man who eats my flesh and drinks my blood enjoys eternal life, and I will raise him up at the last day. My flesh is real food, my blood is real drink. He who eats my flesh, and drinks my blood, lives continually in me, and I in him."[15] The crowd murmured and went away, and some of the disciples deserted.

Wine and oil press (the millstone of the Gospel), Capharnaum

Spring of Mary Magdalene, Magdala, Galilee

The Apostles went to Him and Peter said, "Thou art the Christ, the Son of God."

Jesus answered them, "Have I not chosen all twelve of you? And one of you is a devil . . ."[16]

The site of Capharnaum stretches for a mile or so round the synagogue, but is overgrown with dense brushwood, so that exploration is difficult. All one can say now is that an important lakeside town once existed there, probably with a little harbor to which boats came from various parts of the lake and where also they were no doubt glad to run for shelter from the sudden storms which still occur with alarming speed on the Sea of Galilee.

Two places bear the name of Magdala: one, a squalid site near the shore, where a few huts stand under palm trees; the other more to the south, just off the main road, where a beautiful glasslike spring of water is to be seen. The Magdala of the Gospels, wherever it was, was a prosperous place, one of three towns, according to the Talmud, whose Temple tribute was carried to Jerusalem in wagons. It was also notorious for its vice and some authorities think that the term "the Magdalene" may have been equivalent to "the harlot." There is no scriptural evidence at all, but western Art has stressed that side of the Magdalene's reputation in the days before her repentance. It is curious that Jesus should first have proclaimed His Christhood to a sinful woman in Samaria, and that another woman, whose reputation was not without flaw, should have been granted the first sight of the risen Lord as she sat weeping by the empty tomb.

How frequently the name of Mary occurs in the New Testament: the Blessed Virgin; Mary Magdalene; Mary of Bethany; Mary, mother of Mark; Mary of Cleophas; and Mary, mother of James and John. The name was once considered too sacred for common use. In Siena, during the Middle Ages, no prostitute was allowed to bear it, and in Spain, instead of the name Mary, girls were given names which expressed attributes of the Blessed Virgin, which explains the frequency to this day of such names as Mercedes, Asunción, Concepción and Dolores. The meaning of Mary, in Hebrew Miriam, is believed to be the "wished for," or "longed-for" child.[17]

A steep path leads down among rocks to a little strip of stony shore near the radioactive springs of Tabgha. The water laps stones of black basalt; a grove of eucalyptus trees offers shade; the vegetation is lush, and the fish, of which the lake is full, come close inshore.

Twenty years ago, on a previous visit, I watched a group of Arab fishermen cast their nets at this point and return to shore with *musht*, or St. Peter's Fish, which they cooked over a fire of twigs and offered to travelers on strips of the large circular local bread. Today the Arabs have gone, but the task is still performed by Jewish fishermen. Two kinds of nets are in use: the handnet and the seine or dragnet, which is used by two or more fishermen. The most interesting to watch is the casting of the handnet. The fisherman wades out a few yards from the shore and casts the net so that, as it bells out in the air, the weights with which the edges are sewn hit the water at the same moment and carry the net down, imprisoning any fish in the area. Four

Following page: Casting handnet, Sea of Galilee

or five times we watched the fisherman cast, walking about between each throw, then eventually he drew in his net with five or six large *musht* in it. This is the *chromis simonis,* in whose large mouth the male of the species carries its young. It is said to be the fish in whose mouth St. Peter found the silver coin to pay the Temple pence when, at the bidding of Jesus, he baited his hook and cast it into the water. This, incidentally, is the only reference in the Gospels to line fishing.

The miracle of the loaves and fishes took place at this end of the lake, and a Byzantine church was erected in memory of it on the higher ground at the back of the little bay. The attractive mosaic pavement depicts, lovingly and amusingly, the characteristics of various plump water fowl, and such solemn birds as the stork and the crane. Twenty years ago the pavement was in the open air and covered with sand.

The sand was brushed away by an Arab caretaker for the edification of visitors, then a bucket of water was swept across the pavement to bring out the colors. Most surprisingly, the mosaic has survived this treatment and is now within a church, the Church of the Miracle of the Loaves and Fishes, which is in charge of the Benedictines of Mount Sion.

One always returns to the waterside to reflect that never in history has so much of importance to mankind taken place in so small and so apparently commonplace a spot. Upon those waters Jesus saw Simon, and Simon's brother, Andrew, casting a net into the water. "I will make you fishers of men," he said. So the symbol of the fish and the fisherman passed from Galilee into Christian life. One recalls standing in the chill depths of the Catacombs, holding up a taper to the sign of a fish drawn or painted on the stucco of a tomb by some early Christian in the age of Nero; one remembers that in the recent excavations beneath the nave of St. Peter's this same symbol was found upon a tomb, where "the human soul is typified by a fish and plunged in the waters of Baptism is drawn forth by the Angler, washed and reborn into a new divine life of grace—a positive conception of restoration to a spiritual plane of which the pagan world seems to have had no inkling."[18] Another archaeologist who has studied the street of tombs under St. Peter's comments that "each Christian is miraculously 'fished' by the Divine Fisherman."[19]

Loaves and fishes in handnet, Tabgha, Gal

The Jews always loved acrostics and when it was discovered that from the initial letters of the Greek word for a fish, *ichthus,* it was possible to compose the sentence *Iesous CHristos THeou Uios Soter* ("Jesus Christ, Son of God, Saviour") the fish became the universal sign whereby Christians recognized each other and the symbol with which they expressed their faith in the Fisherman of Galilee. "We little Fishes," said Tertullian, in his treatise on Baptism, "are born in water"; and the word *piscina,* from the Latin word for a fish, was given to the font.

One therefore looks with awe upon these fish that are drawn out of the Lake of Galilee every day and roasted on stones for the visitor. There seems to be something sacramental in such food in such a place. Here, too, is the spot, above all others, to read that superb piece of writing in which St. John describes the appearance of Christ after the Resurrection. It is a picture drawn in the half light of morning, a study in atmosphere and the economy of words:

"Jesus appeared to his disciples again afterwards, at the sea of Tiberias, and this is how he appeared to them. Simon Peter was there, and with him were Thomas, who is also called Didymus, and Nathanael, from Cana of Galilee, and the sons of Zebedee, and two more of his disciples. Simon Peter told them, I am going out fishing; and they said, We, too, will go with thee. So they went out and embarked on the boat, and all that night they caught nothing. But when morning came, there was Jesus standing on the shore; only the disciples did not know that it was Jesus. Have you caught anything, friends, Jesus asked them, to season your bread with? And when they answered No, he said to them, Cast to the right of the boat, and you will have a catch. So they cast the net, and found before long they had no strength to haul it in, such a shoal of fish was in it. Whereupon the disciple whom Jesus loved said to Peter, It is the Lord. And Simon Peter, hearing him say it was the Lord, girded up the fisherman's coat, which was all he wore, and sprang into the sea. The other disciples followed in the boat (they were not far from land, only some hundred yards away), dragging their catch in the net behind them. So they went ashore, and found a charcoal fire made there, with fish and bread cooking on it. Bring some of the fish you have just caught, said Jesus to them: and

Church of Beatitudes, Mount of Beatitudes, Galilee

Simon Peter, going on board, hauled in the net to land. It was loaded with great fish, a hundred and fifty-three of them; and with all that number the net had not broken. When Jesus said to them, Come and break your fast, none of the disciples ventured to ask him, Who art thou? knowing well that it was the Lord. So Jesus came up and took bread, which he gave to them, and fish as well. Thus Jesus appeared to his disciples a third time after his rising from the dead."[20]

A beautiful chapel above the lake is the work of Barluzzi. It occupies a position upon a level hill to the north, upon the traditional

Following page: Preaching from the Mount of Beatitudes, Galilee

Mount of the Beatitudes. Like Barluzzi's other churches, this is an architectural essay in atmosphere and symbolism.

It is an octagonal building, to symbolize the eight Beatitudes, one of which is inscribed on each of the windows. The walls are of gray marble, and the dome above the altar glitters with gold mosaic. This unusual building was completed in 1938.

The chapel is surrounded by an attractive columned portico and commands one of the best views of the lake, which is seen stretching southward almost to Tiberias. Holy sites are of two kinds: those shrines and altars which have been sanctified by the faith and devotion of the centuries, and those which remain as God made them and as our Lord saw them. If the Apostles stood today upon the Mount of Beatitudes they would at once recognize the scene, though the busy cities and towns of Galilee have now vanished. The mountains are the same, the water is as blue, the birds sing as they used to do, the same little black and white kingfishers dart above the streams of Tabgha, the same flowers are growing on the hills. Sometimes the pilgrim may feel nearer to Jesus under the sky of Galilee than in the darkness of a grotto, no matter how holy and how revered.

Possibly only a saint could stand upon the Mount of Beatitudes without experiencing a twinge of uneasiness; for this is the scene of that code of conduct—that counsel of perfection—which sounds so easy but is, really, the reversal of all worldly standards. Yet upon this hill those thoughts were sown in the mind of man which could bring heaven to earth.

Bishop Sheen has said: "The Beatitudes cannot be taken alone: they are not ideals; they are hard facts and realities inseparable from the Cross of Calvary. What He taught was self-crucifixion: to love those who hate us; to pluck out eyes and cut off arms in order to prevent sinning; to be clean on the inside when the passions clamor for satisfaction on the outside; to forgive those who would put us to death; to overcome evil with good; to bless those who curse us; to stop mouthing freedom until we have justice, truth and love of God in our hearts as the condition of freedom; to live in the world and still keep oneself unpolluted from it; to deny ourselves sometimes legitimate pleasures in order the better to crucify our egotism——all this is to sentence the old man in us to death."[21]

And another learned commentator has written: "According to Jesus' teaching and example, a man's success or failure is to be judged not by the amount of money he can accumulate, or by the amount of social distinction he can command, or by the extent of his intellectual or official achievements; but rather by the essential character which he fashions within himself, and by the service which he renders to his fellow-men. In the Beatitudes Jesus calls men away from the superficial tests and standards which so commonly prevail, to a criterion which concerns the real nature of man, is equally just to all, and stands in relation not alone to the few years of a man's present existence, but to the whole of his eternal career. . . . The man, woman or child, who sincerely, persistently aspires and strives to attain to the character and to perform the services described in the Beatitudes will not fail of Christianity either in knowledge or achievement."[22]

In the hospice on the hill behind the chapel, Franciscan Sisters of the Immaculate Heart of Mary greet the tired pilgrim and place food and drink before him with that kindness and that sense of humble service which are among the Beatitudes.

IV THE TRANSFIGURATION

ON THE WAY from the Sea of Galilee to Nazareth the road passes through an untidy little village, once called Cana and now known as Kafr Kannà, where Jesus attended a wedding feast with His mother. The first of the miracles, the turning of the water into wine, captured the imagination of the first pilgrims to an extraordinary degree, and in early days a large basilica was built over the house of the wedding feast. St. Willibald, who was there in 754, wrote: "There is to be seen here a large church; on the altar is to be found one of the six pitchers which the Saviour had filled with water which was changed into wine."[23] Today the large church has vanished, but signs of it are to be seen in the crypt of the present Franciscan church, where also may be seen the same Jewish pitcher noted so long ago by St. Willibald.

A few miles south of Nazareth one comes to Naim, where a Franciscan chapel commemorates the raising of the widow's son. When Jesus stopped a funeral procession here, the body was no doubt being taken to the tombs which can still be seen nearby. And from Naim the land is dominated by the immense smooth dome of a mountain of great character and importance: this is Tabor of which the Psalmist wrote: "The north wind and the south are of thy fashioning; thy name wakes the glad echoes of Thabor and Hermon."[24]

It does indeed appear as though Tabor exults over the well-tended landscape above which it is lifted triumphantly against the sky. The road winds round and about the mountain until the traveler is deposited, some nineteen hundred feet above the sea, upon a summit occupied by a Franciscan church, a monastery and a mass of crusading ruins. A tradition going back to the time of St. Silvia of Aquitania claims Mount Tabor to be the scene of our Lord's Transfiguration.

Ancient water jug in Church of Cana, Galilee

Roof of church at Cana of Galilee

The church is by Barluzzi and here again that versatile genius has created a building full of symbolism and beauty. The history of the site, which the Franciscans have redeemed from its astonishing changes of fortune, should be known to every pilgrim. There was a church here in the fourth century; in the sixth there were three. The Moslem invasion swept them away, but the Crusades restored them and Benedictines occupied the mountain. They held it until 1142, when they were massacred; but Benedictines were back in 1183 and remained until the defeat of the Crusaders, when they were forced to leave.

The Sultan of Damascus then built a fortress on Tabor to control the approach to Acre. In 1217 a powerful army of Christian knights

Chapel, Naim

scaled the mountain, but were driven off; and in the following year the Sultan dismantled the fortress to deny it to the Christians. It then disappeared from history for thirty-seven years, to emerge as a stronghold of the Knights of St. John, who rebuilt the churches and the Benedictine abbey. In 1263 that remarkable character who began life as a slave, the Mameluke Sultan of Egypt, Baibars, drove the Christians from the mountain and razed all their buildings to the ground. Mount Tabor then disappears for three and a half centuries. When it emerges again, the Franciscans have established a humble foothold there. In

1888 the first American pilgrimage to be organized to the Holy Land made a vow to rebuild the church, but this was opposed by the Turkish Government of the day. So matters rested until the first World War, when the Turks were driven out of Palestine by the British, and, under the British Mandate, the fulfillment of the "American Vow" was at last a possibility. The foundation stone was laid in 1919 and the Church of the Transfiguration was dedicated in 1924.

As usual, Barluzzi has wonderfully linked this church with the three churches of Tabor. They were inspired by St. Peter's wish to erect three "arbours" during the Transfiguration, one for our Lord, one for Moses, and one for Elias. When the three disciples awakened from sleep and saw the Lord transfigured, His garments as white as snow, St. Peter said, "Master, it is well that we should be here; let us make three arbours in this place, one for thee, one for Moses, and one for Elias. But he spoke at random: and even as he said it, a cloud formed, overshadowing them; they saw those others disappear into the cloud, and were terrified. And a voice came from the cloud, This is my beloved Son; to him, then, listen."[25]

A mystical light glows in this building from the alabaster windows, of which Barluzzi is so fond, and you can see the entire church at a glance from the door. There is an upper church with its altar and, immediately below, a broad stairway leads to a crypt which preserves

Entrance, Basilica of Transfiguration, Mount Tabor, Galilee

the curve of the Confessional of the earlier church discovered during the excavations. The semi-dome of the upper church is decorated with a beautiful mosaic from the Vatican factory, showing Jesus levitated in a glow of supernatural light, "His face shining like the sun, and His garments becoming white as snow,"[26] while in the background, in the clouds, are Moses and Elias; in the foreground are the awed and wondering figures of Peter, John and James.

On each side of the main entrance are chapels dedicated to Moses and Elias, the "Arbours," now formed of the stone of the Mount of Transfiguration, to fulfill St. Peter's "random" wish. Many will think this Basilica to be Barluzzi's masterpiece. He has departed entirely from the tradition of the Roman basilica, and one is reminded of those massive pre-Byzantine Syrian churches round Antioch which are so impressive, even in their decay.

A friar bent down and pulled up a trap door in the crypt, exposing a rough area of the mountain top.

"The Mountain of the Transfiguration," he said.

From the rocks round the church the view is stupendous. Away to the north, sometimes obscured, but often rising above the cloud, are

Basilica of Transfiguration, Mount Tabor

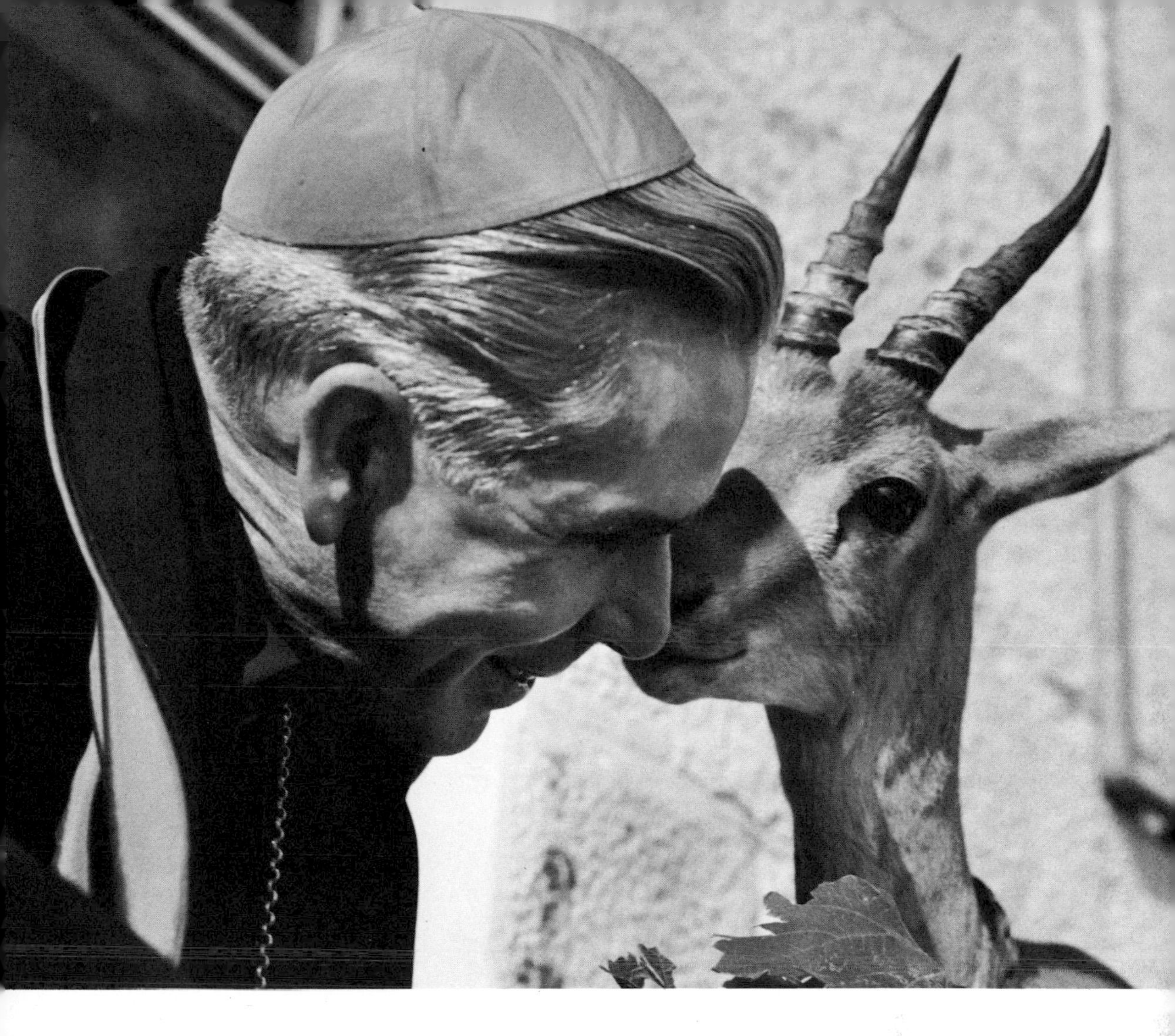

the snows of Hermon; to the northeast is a blue spoonful of the Sea of Galilee; to the east is a savage, tumbled mountainscape, sometimes as blue as a gentian—the wild, desolate Hauran beyond Jordan. Southward and westward is the plain where the armies of Debbora defeated the iron, scythe-wheeled chariots of Sisera, which in those days must have been the equivalent of an armored division.

We had luncheon with the kindly Franciscans in the hospice, and afterwards a tame gazelle was introduced to us, which ran and leapt upon its thin and graceful legs to the delight of the friars, condescending to nibble a few leaves, then, stiffening with ancestral fears, leapt over a chair or a table, watched balefully by the hospice cat.

When they came down from the Mount of Transfiguration Jesus said to His disciples, "The Son of Man is soon to be betrayed into the hands of men."[27]

The Way of the Cross began.

Ruins of Caesarea, seat of Pontius Pilate

4

The Way of the Cross

Site of the Temple, Mosque of Omar and Dome of the Rock, Jerusalem

I JERUSALEM

At first one is inclined to think that the Arab city of Old Jerusalem is unchanged. The same vaulted streets, like the naves and transepts of ruined abbeys, are thronged with the familiar crowd of Arabs, Greeks, Armenians, Syrians and Copts; the hundreds of congested little lock-up booths and shops still line the streets; and tireless hawkeyed merchants still ply the stranger with offers of embroidery, jewelry and scent.

They give the impression, just as they used to do, that commerce is a merry game; and they continue to despise the Westerner who pays what he is asked, and so denies them the chief pleasure of trade: the mental exercise of bargaining.

It is still necessary to stand aside, while descending the steep ramps of David Street, to allow a laden camel to advance, or to give room to the bent and staggering figure of some Arab Atlas with a wardrobe or a piano upon his back. There are still thousands of dark little shops where men beat copper, or set moonstones in crusading crosses, or cook nuts and honey cakes; the same languid Arab moves through the crowds, leading a goat by the ear; the pet lamb with a blue ribbon round its neck still goes for a walk with children; the same piercing Arab music issues from loudspeakers, and the singer's voice is still suddenly amputated on his highest note, as if an executioner had entered the recording studio and had slain the vocalist.

Through the crowd pass those unchanging figures: a Greek priest, with patriarchal beard, wearing dusty black robes and a rimless black hat; the spectacled Armenian beneath a black triangular hood; and the Franciscan, who, even if swarthy and Latin, appears white and rosy and European in that dark assembly.

The medieval streets, too steep and narrow for wheels, penetrate the ancient labyrinth, half in sunlight, half in shadow; huge nail-studded doors, like those of a fortress are set in uncompromising walls and admit to unexpected scenes: Spanish sisters serving pilgrims the kind of civilized luncheon you get in Granada or Santiago; a group of oriental prelates seated upon red and gold chairs, eating rose-petal jam and sipping coffee; a number of monks, twenty feet down in a dusty pit, excavating some building of Gospel times.

All this is the same. But there are also changes. Old Jerusalem is now a frontier and from the western angle of the wall, were you allowed to go there, you would look down into No Man's Land and Israel. The Moslem sentries man the medieval wall as if in the time of Suleiman the Magnificent. There is a memory of the British rule in the smart uniforms of the police with their spiked khaki helmets, and also in the phenomenal cleanliness of the streets.

Amusingly enough, the muezzin, that unchanging figure of the East, has proved susceptible to change. Many a muezzin no longer mounts his minaret, but chants the call to prayer into a microphone at the base of his tower, which relays it by loud speakers from the platform above. Strangest of all, there are no Jews at the Wailing Wall. The gigantic blocks of honey-colored stone—part of the western platform of Herod's Temple—have even been plucked of their innumerable prayers and pleas, written on parchment, and once thrust by the orthodox Jews into every hole and cranny. There are no Jews in Old Jerusalem for the first time since the age of Hadrian.

The stately social engagements of Jerusalem continue as usual: receptions where the Rev. Father Custos of the Holy Land receives the Diplomatic Corps; elaborately courteous occasions when oriental

Wailing Wall, Jerusa

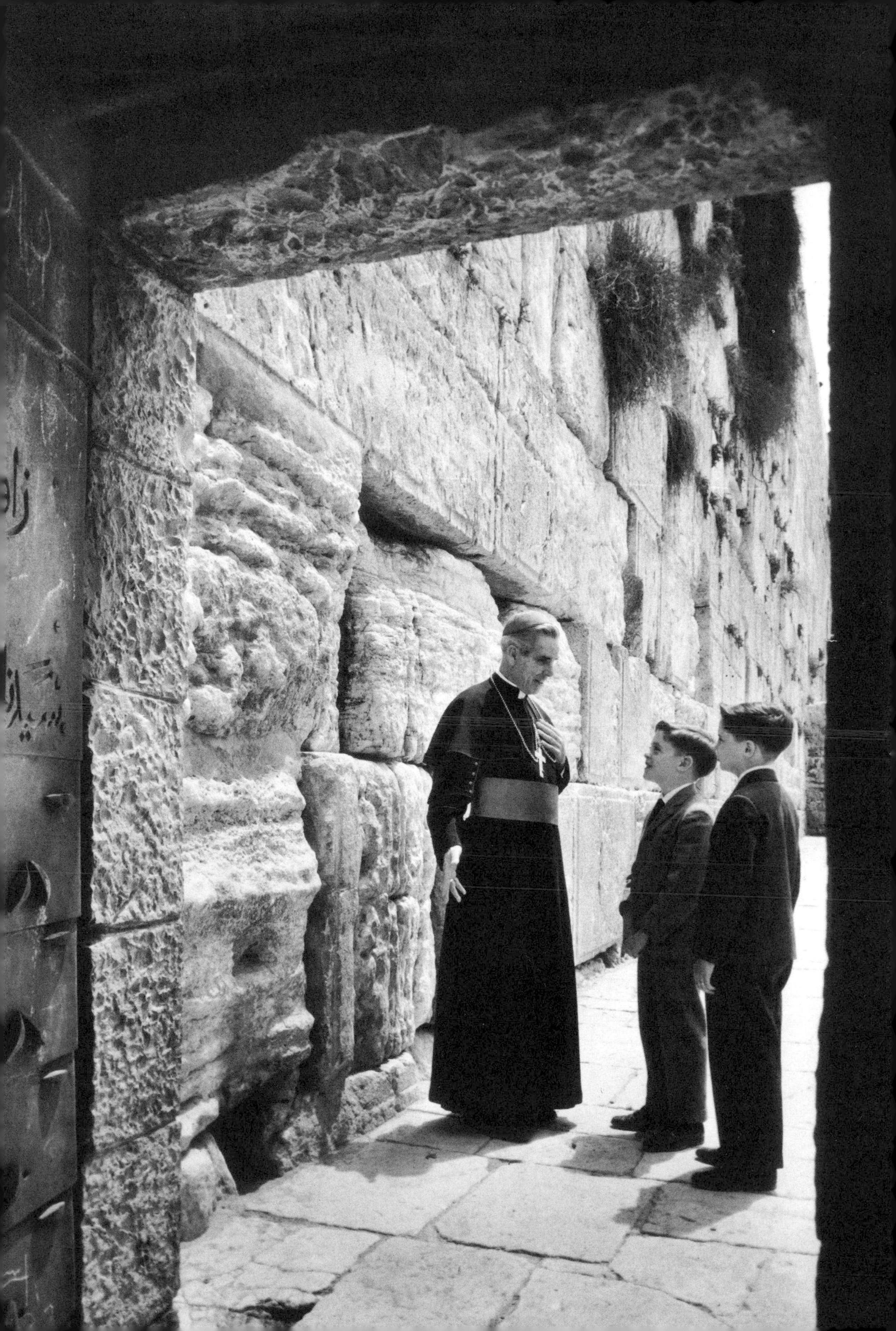

Golden Gate from Temple site, Jerusalem

patriarchs, seated in a circle, nod their immense white beards and eat sweet cakes. Slightly more modern in atmosphere was a reception given in an hotel by a government official, where the guests were closely scrutinized on entering by security forces, and watched throughout the proceedings by police armed with Sten guns. It transpired that a plot against the life of our host had just been discovered!

II THE HOUSE OF THE LAST SUPPER

JUST OUTSIDE the southwestern wall of Jerusalem is the House of the Last Supper—the Cenacle—which, after the Holy Sepulchre itself, is the most sacred site in the Holy Land. Though within hailing distance, it is in Israel and separated from the Old City by the barbed wire of No Man's Land.

In former days one passed through the Jaffa Gate (now blocked up) and a few minutes walking brought one to this building, then a mosque. There was an even shorter cut, if you knew it, in a door at the end of a passage, which someone was always willing to unlock, and, there, only a few yards away, was the Cenacle.

In order to see the Cenacle today it is necessary to wind up one's affairs in Jordan and enter Israel; for once departed, one may return no more. The only persons who may pass to and fro between the two countries, with the permission of the Jordan Government, are officials of the United Nations and the heads of religious bodies who have responsibilities on both sides of the frontier. Pilgrims are permitted to cross and return only at Christmas and Easter.

There is a curious technique about this departure: one must never mention in Jordan that one is crossing into Israel. It is a polite fiction that Israel does not exist. One talks about "crossing over," or going to "the other side," or "you know where," or any other acceptable euphemism which avoids direct mention of the Jewish State.

The only direct exit from Jordan to Israel is by way of the Mandelbaum Gate. There is no gate there; and where Mandelbaum was would be difficult to say. The name is that of a merchant who once dwelt in one of the shell-shattered buildings which line No Man's Land at this point. There is an Arab police post and a frontier pole across the road. Fifty yards away is another frontier pole and a Jewish police post. Perhaps because one is technically disintegrating, vanishing officially, going nowhere, becoming a kind of *jinn*, the Arab police are extremely friendly, and shake hands before they lift the pole. You now walk across No Man's Land, noting the barbed wire, the old sandbags, the destroyed buildings, the crazily poised fireplace in a sliced house, and, covered by the machine guns of Jordan and also those of Israel, you arrive at another shed, where you materialize again as a traveler with a passport. The Jewish police and customs officials welcome you with official cordiality, and wave you on into New Jerusalem.

Here is a modern city with big public buildings, offices and flats, traffic police, a suburban bus service, neon lights, and a teeming population drawn from Europe and America, which appears full of confidence in itself. It is an odd experience to sit on the terrace of the big hotel and to reflect that the crenellated walls of Old Jerusalem nearby conceal a sentry who would have to be a particularly bad shot to be unable to pick off a tourist or, if a marksman, to shatter his teacup.

It is strange to see the ancient Hebrew alphabet written on shop fronts and at street corners. Calligraphically, it is less attractive than Arabic with its many pleasing whirls and curves, and it does not enlarge well. The ponderous, heavy black symbols appear rather ominous, so that any mundane inscription written up on a draper's shop might be something threatening like "an eye for an eye." It may be that one is conditioned to associate Hebrew with prophetic utterances, and one is therefore slightly shocked to learn that a word, which looks as if it ought to spell Moses, means "aspirin."

One of the most attractive features of Israeli Jerusalem is the great number of small but admirable bookshops. Also attractive are the many talented and efficient persons one meets in the course of a day.

One of the longest and strongest traditions in Christianity is that the House of the Last Supper occupied the steep rocky ledge now outside the present wall of Jerusalem at a point opposite the Sion Gate.

Cenacle, Mount Sion, Jerusaler

In the time of Christ this district was enclosed by the wall, which has been traced some way to the south of it.

The Cenacle, or Cenaculum (Latin: an eating room or upper story) must have been a building of considerable size: on one occasion the Upper Room held a hundred and twenty people. It was a house with a flat roof like those seen everywhere in hot countries, where it is pleasant to eat in the cool of the evening. An attractive conjecture for which there is no scriptural authority is that the house belonged to "Mary, mother of John also called Mark," and that it became the meeting-place of the Apostles after the Ascension. "About a hundred and twenty were gathered there" when St. Peter cast lots to decide the successor to Judas. In addition to "the brethren," a considerable number of people lived in the house, including the Blessed Virgin.

To this building St. Peter sped in haste when he was delivered from prison. The owner employed a young maidservant named Rhoda—a common slave name—who was so excited when she heard St. Peter's voice asking to be let in, that she rushed away without opening the door and told those inside the house that St. Peter was there. They refused to believe her and called her mad. Then, rushing to the door, on which St. Peter was still knocking, they admitted him. But he did not stay. He asked them to tell the brethren of his escape and "went elsewhere." The implication is, perhaps, that this house was too well known, and Peter was anxious to remove himself from the jurisdiction of Herod.

It is a tradition that the "upper room" of the Last Supper and the "upper room" of Acts were the same place, and no other site than the Cenacle has ever been put forward. This building escaped the destruction of Jerusalem under Titus and was a church, says St. Epiphanius, when Hadrian surveyed the ruins in A.D. 135 and decided to rebuild the city. St. Cyril of Jerusalem (A.D. 350) speaks of the "upper church of the Apostles where the Holy Ghost descended upon them," which was upon Mount Sion. Thus the Cenacle is the oldest Christian church known to history.

The first pilgrims saw a small building on the site and in the time of the Crusaders a large basilica was served by canons regular of St.

Augustine. The fortunes of the church fluctuated with those of the other holy sites, but the most tragic of its vicissitudes occurred as recently as the sixteenth century when the Franciscans, then in occupation, were expelled owing to the plotting of Jews and Moslems. It was said that the Christians were keeping secret the tomb of David which they had discovered in the lower portion of the Cenacle. The Sultan was persuaded to issue an order for the expulsion of the Franciscans, which took place in 1551.

If the Jews hoped to claim the supposed tomb of David, they were disappointed. The Moslems took over the beautiful Franciscan church, split it up in various ways and made a mosque out of the "upper room." This was in use until 1948 when, with the partition of Jerusalem, the Moslems left and the Cenacle became Israeli territory. Twenty years ago the Christian visitor was hurried through the mosque and was not permitted to kneel there or to display any sign of devotion; and the lower room, the tomb of David, and the traditional site of the room where Jesus washed the feet of His disciples, was locked and barred.

Today a long flight of steps leads to Mount Sion and from the top you can see a stretch of the immense golden wall of old Jerusalem and the roofs of the buildings which cluster between the Sion and the Jaffa Gates. You could shout across to anyone there, and the story is told of an impatient tourist who recently, though warned not to do so, jumped into No Man's Land to cross the few yards into the Old City and was promptly shot dead.

The road to the top of Sion is now the way of Jewish pilgrimage to the tomb of David. On public holidays great numbers of Jews, carrying flags which bear the Star of David, climb Mount Sion, some as if they were going to the Wailing Wall and others to spend the day and picnic there. A notice at the top of the steps bears these words: "Attention visitors: You are on the holy Mount Zion. Please wear your headgear and be modestly dressed; we will lend you skull caps and head shawls, free of charge. The Mount Zion Committee."

The mount is occupied by the remains of the Crusading Franciscan basilica: weed-grown courtyards, beautiful gateways with dog-tooth molding, and vaulted corridors, are permeated by an air of decay and abandonment. It is now possible to enter a dark vault where, behind an iron railing, the sarcophagus of David may be discerned. This was the sight once so jealously guarded by the Moslems from Christian eyes and, now, by one of the strange reversals of fortune so typical of the Holy Land, a Jewish shrine.

The hilltop is occupied by two modern buildings. One is the Benedictine Abbey of the Dormition, founded by German monks about fifty years ago. The abbot exercises jurisdiction over Weston Priory in the Green Mountains of Southern Vermont, thus forging a link between Mount Sion and the United States. The monks also serve the

Church of the Dormition, Mount Sion

Church of the Miracle of the Loaves and Fishes at Tabgha, on the lakeside of Galilee.

The abbey church is one of the most beautiful sanctuaries built recently in the Holy Land. It is erected upon the site of the Byzantine church of Our Lady of Mount Sion, and commemorates the place where, in the opinion of many, the Blessed Virgin fell peacefully asleep at an advanced age. The monks took us down to the crypt, a solemn and majestic rotunda, which is occupied by a life-sized figure of our Lady, lying with folded hands.

The second building is the chapel of the convent of St. Francis, which dates from 1936. Father Eugene Hoade, whose admirable guide to the Holy Land is well known to pilgrims, has described, in a brief history of the Franciscans and the Cenacle,[1] how the friars managed to buy this site and so return to Mount Sion for the first time since the sixteenth century. "It may be the dawn of better days," comments the writer; and one hopes so. It is touching to notice that, knowing the pilgrim would wish to be as near as possible to the Cenacle, the friars have filled the window behind the altar with clear glass through which the Cenacle is seen a short distance away.

The Cenacle itself is a deplorable sight. You approach the "upper room" by a flight of steps which leads into a roofless anteroom, probably shattered by the 1948 fighting, beyond which is the now vacant mosque. It is part of the old church, and dates from the fourteenth century. Two columns in the center of the building support pointed vaulting, while half columns are built into the walls. A *mihrab,* or prayer niche, has been built into the south wall, and the little chapel is lighted by pointed windows whose glass has been broken. The columns have been daubed with cheap paint and the place is the picture of abandonment and neglect. The Israelis have said they plan to take steps to prevent its further deterioration; thus far, nothing has been done. But at least the pilgrim may kneel here for the first time since 1552. As he does so, he will reflect that a long tradition links this site with the house of the Last Supper; the house of the Miracle of Pentecost; the house of the first Christian community after the Ascension.

"And he said to them, I have longed and longed to share this paschal meal with you before my passion; I tell you, I shall not eat it again, till it finds its fulfilment in the kingdom of God. And He took a cup, and blessed it, and said, Take this and share it among you; I tell you, I shall not drink of the fruit of the vine again, till the kingdom of God has come. Then He took bread, and blessed and broke it, and gave it to them, saying, This is my body, given for you; do this for a commemoration of me. And so with the cup, when supper was ended, This cup, He said, is the new testament, in my blood which is to be shed for you. And now, the hand of my betrayer rests upon this table, at my side. The Son of Man goes on His way, for so it has been ordained. . . ."[2]

In this poor, abandoned place Christ gave the first Communion and instituted the mystery of His Church, and the pilgrim looks round at the Mother and Head of all Churches, thinking that "where two or three are gathered together in my name" is something of the holy Cenacle.

Mount of Olives with Gethsemane in foreground, Jerusalem

Entrance to Grotto of Betrayal, Gethsemane, Jerusalem

III GETHSEMANE

THE EASTERN wall overhangs the Valley of the Kidron, and on the slope opposite is the Mount of Olives. Low down on the hill is a small, walled enclosure in which eight venerable olive trees are growing. This is the Garden of Gethsemane.

It has been claimed that these immense trees are those which were actually growing in the time of Christ; and this is possible, for the olive appears to be practically immortal and to send out a shoot when almost moribund. It is not, however, probable. Josephus tells us that when Titus stationed two legions on the Mount of Olives in A.D. 70, he leveled all walls and cut down all trees to prevent the Jews from using them as cover.

The eight aged trees seem to have more in common with the mineral than the vegetable kingdom: they might be monoliths in which a few green shoots have lodged. Yet, strange to say, they still bear fruit and the Franciscans still press oil from them. The stones are as precious as the oil. They are made into rosaries which are reserved for the Father Custodian of the Holy Land. The Franciscans took possession of Gethsemane in 1681. For many years they left the Garden as they had found it, and as some would still prefer to see it: a rough, uncultivated portion of the Mount of Olives, surrounded by a cactus hedge. In 1848 it was, however, necessary for legal reasons to enclose it with a wall, and gradually the idea of cultivating the Garden took shape. Twenty years ago, one seems to recollect, the Garden site was much simpler: a few box hedges and some flowers in pots. This has now given way to a brilliant little garden which would be entirely charming in any other situation. Sweet William, phlox, lobelia, nasturtiums, geraniums and pansies, are beautiful in one's own garden, but are they, after all, suitable for Gethsemane? On the other hand, in what other way can a garden praise God save with flowers?

In the Church of All Nations, Barluzzi has designed the darkest of all his churches: some say it is too dark. The light filters through bluish alabaster, and it is some time before one can see anything. His object was to interpret the gloom and sadness of the Passion and the darkness that was to pass across the face of the earth, just as at Bethlehem he created a church full of light and joyfulness, and at Ain Karem one full of dignity and clarity, and upon Mount Tabor a church whose mystical beauty rises against a background of the sky.

During the work of excavation traces were found of two former churches on the site, and of the greatest interest were the remains of the fourth century building mentioned by St. Jerome and visited by St. Silvia. It was seen that a large rectangular piece of the rock of

Garden of Gethsemane, Jerusalem

Rock of Christ's Agony, Church of All Nations, Gethsemane, Jerusalem

Gethsemane had been preserved in front of the altar of the old church, and Barluzzi took delight in restoring it to this position in the new one. When their eyes become accustomed to the darkness, pilgrims see this impressive dome of rock exposed before the altar, and they can now revere it as their predecessors did so many centuries ago.

Those who have been privileged to enter the Garden of Gethsemane by the light of the full moon carry the memory all their lives. It was at such a moment that Jesus, standing among the olive trees in the moonlight, said to Peter and the Sons of Zebedee: "My soul . . . is ready to die with sorrow; do you abide here and watch with me."[3]

He went apart to pray, and soon lights were seen, and approaching footsteps sounded along the stony path to the Garden.

Altar of Betrayal, Grotto, Gethseman

Good Friday on the Via Dolorosa, Jerusalem

IV VIA DOLOROSA

We were shown the excavations now being made by the White Fathers upon what is believed to be the Pool of Bethesda, in the grounds of St. Anne's Church, near St. Stephen's Gate. First we admired the massive church, so like a great Gothic shrine, which was one of the few Christian buildings not entirely gutted by the Persians in 614. It has had an extraordinary history: a Christian church; a Moslem theological college under Saladin; then centuries of varied humiliation and neglect, ending in a surprising resurrection in 1856, when the Sultan of Turkey gave the building, by that time a tottering shell, to France in return for help during the Crimean War.

The busy scene nearby, where the White Fathers are revealing what is almost certainly the Pool of Bethesda, was one of dusty confusion. We looked down into a huge pit, twenty feet or more in depth, in whose sides we could read the history of Jerusalem in protruding pottery and other fragments. At the bottom of the excavation were columns and walls which might be those of the place where Jesus healed the cripple. The Pool was divided into two portions and was approached by five porches; and these are among the objects which the excavators are bringing to light.

Pool of Bethesda, Jerusalem

No one had any satisfactory explanation of the mystery of the "troubling" or "bubbling up" of the waters at intervals, which was regarded by cripples and invalids as the divinely appointed moment to plunge in.[4] The Bordeaux Pilgrim, who saw the twin pools in 333, wrote that "these pools have water which, when agitated, is of a kind of red color," obviously the same place mentioned in the next century by Eucherius, who said that "one pool is for the most part filled by winter rains, the other is discolored by reddish waters." Modern authorities are hardly more informative. Edersheim says: "The bubbling of the water was, of course, due not to supernatural but to physical causes. Such intermittent springs are not uncommon, and to this day the so-called Fountain of the Virgin in Jerusalem exhibits the same phenomenon." George Adam Smith thought the movement might be that of a syphonic spring, and he mentions that the water of the Pool of Siloam was also disturbed at intervals by the intermittent rush from Gihon.

The Franciscans have their Biblical School and Museum a few yards along the Via Dolorosa. The objects are all beautifully displayed and are of great interest to every student of New Testament times. Father Augustine Spijkerman, the curator, placed in our hands the type of coin paid to Judas, which was not, as once believed, the Jewish shekel, but the silver shekel of Tyre, a coin about the size of an English florin, but much better looking. It is entirely Hellenistic in design and shows, on one side, the head of the Phoenician deity, Melkarth, and, on the other, the eagle of Tyre. He also produced the tribute money, which was the coin St. Peter found in the mouth of the fish. This was the stater of Antioch, which bore the head of Augustus on one side and the City Goddess of Antioch on the other, with the words, "year twenty-eight of the Victory," or twenty-eight years after Augustus had defeated Antony and Cleopatra at Actium.

We spent some fascinating moments with a plaster model of Jerusalem as it was in the time of Christ. This gives a good idea of the city and, what is so important for any reconstruction of the Trial of our Lord and the Crucifixion, the position of the chief buildings and their relationship to Golgotha.

Coin of time of Betrayal, Franciscan Museum, Via Dolorosa, Jerusalem

Model of Fortress of Antonia, Convent of Sisters of Sion, Via Dolorosa, Jerusalem

V THE LITHOSTROTOS

THE Ecce Homo Arch, which spans the Via Dolorosa, could not look less Roman. It appears to be entirely Arab, and above the road it contains a small room whose barred windows might be those of a harem or a prison. As a matter of fact, they are neither: the room is full of papers and magazines which belong to Sheik Mousa Boukhary, a schoolmaster, who is also muezzin of the adjacent Boukharian mosque. He courteously offered us the use of the room for the Good Friday processions.

But the arch is unquestionably Roman, and it was believed in the Middle Ages that two stones in or near it were those upon which Jesus and Pilate stood when Pilate pronounced the words "*Ecce homo*"—"Behold the man." To realize that the arch is a part of the usual Roman gateway, which had a large central opening for wheeled traffic, flanked by two smaller arches on each side, for foot passengers, it is necessary to visit the neighboring convent of the Dames de Sion, where the northern arch of the two smaller gates is to be seen in the chapel. It was once believed that the Ecce Homo Arch was standing at the time of Christ, but some modern authorities think it may have been one of the gates of Aelia Capitolina.

As we glanced down from the little room, we saw the narrow Via Dolorosa packed from wall to wall with pilgrims visiting the fourteen Stations of the Cross which lead to Calvary within the Church of the Holy Sepulchre. All nations were represented in the crowds which passed for hours beneath us, some carrying wooden crosses whose weight was shared by monks or by pilgrims.

Whether the Via Dolorosa is really the Way of the Cross depends upon the position of the "Praetorium" where our Lord was tried before Pilate. It is a word translated by Msgr. Knox as "court of the palace," though it stands as "Praetorium" in the Westminster version of St. Mark.[5] In this place was a raised pavement upon which Pilate placed his magisterial chair known, according to St. John, as the "*Lithostrotos*" or, in Hebrew, "*Gabbatha.*"[6] Some few years ago a large stretch of this pavement, which lies to the north and south of the Ecce Homo Arch, was uncovered in circumstances which were remarkable and touching.

In the middle of the last century, Father Marie Alphonse Ratisbonne, a converted Jew who had helped to found a community in France for the conversion of Jews, arrived as a pilgrim in Palestine. He felt so attracted to Jerusalem, and was so convinced that the Virgin had reserved some holy site for him to uncover and restore, that he took up residence there in 1856. Four French nuns came out to live in poverty and in humble quarters, while Father Ratisbonne walked about Jerusalem praying that some site might be shown to him where he could found a convent.

One day, while passing near the Ecce Homo Arch, he met a dragoman named Matthew who had been his guide when he was a pilgrim. He confessed his longings to this man, who said that Father Marie had no need to look any further than the place where he was standing: and he pointed to the ruins which at that date lay to the north of the arch. The priest asked timidly whether a Christian would be allowed to acquire such a site, for Jerusalem was then Turkish and the district was full of fanatical Moslems and dervishes. However, Matthew

Lithostrotos, Convent of Sisters of Sion, Jerusalem

thought that such a purchase might be arranged, and, together, they climbed over the wall and investigated the ruins. While there Father Marie was conscious of the figure of our Lord crowned with thorns and bleeding; and, falling upon his knees, he promised Him that he would not rest until His will had been done.

In 1857 the site was acquired and, with the help of the four sisters, Father Marie cleared away the ruins to discover beneath them the small northern arch of the Roman gate, which he concealed within a little oratory. He had to behave with the utmost caution, and it was not until 1858 that he ventured to say Mass there. He has described how, at four o'clock in the morning on January 20th, he led the way, holding a lantern, while the faithful sisters followed, each one carrying concealed in her habit the vessels and the vestments for the holy sacrifice. The Mass was whispered in the little oratory in circumstances which reminded the good Father of the primitive church and the Catacombs. So affected were the sisters that, at the moment of Holy Communion, they were inspired to renew their vows, which they pronounced with invincible devotion. The priest and the nuns then came out into the still dark Via Dolorosa; and four years later the Convent of the Dames de Sion was built.[7]

We crossed the road and entered the convent. From the roof we enjoyed a superb view of Jerusalem and the Temple area, now the Mosque of the Dome of the Rock. We could look down upon the mighty paved courtyard and see figures moving there, and it was not difficult to cast the mind back to Roman times and to understand how, from the ramparts of the Fortress of Antonia, Pilate's sentries had kept watch upon the Jews.

Under the guidance of Sister Ita we descended beneath the convent and saw that the Dames de Sion draw water from the same cisterns used in the time of Pilate; then, going down a flight of steps, we came in sight of the Lithostrotos. Like anything which was meant to stand in daylight and is now condemned by time to lie in darkness beneath a roof, the place affects one strangely: to see gutters made so long ago to carry off the rains that fell on Jerusalem in Gospel days gave one an awesome impression of the passing of time.

The courtyard is nearly two hundred feet long and about a hundred and fifty feet wide, and it is believed that it was the entrance to the Fortress of Antonia. The stones are enormous, and, indeed, the pavement has the look of a giant's cellar. Some of the stones are three feet square, and all are from twelve to eighteen inches thick.

Sister Ita pointed out to us the transverse fluting made, it is thought, to prevent the horses of the Roman cavalry from slipping, and even more interesting were the curious squares and circles cut in the stones for games like tic-tac-toe, made nineteen centuries ago by soldiers, or by those who waited outside the Praetorium for justice.

If this is indeed the Lithostrotos mentioned by St. John, it has known the footsteps of Christ.

Fourth Station of the Cross, Via Dolorosa, Jerusalem

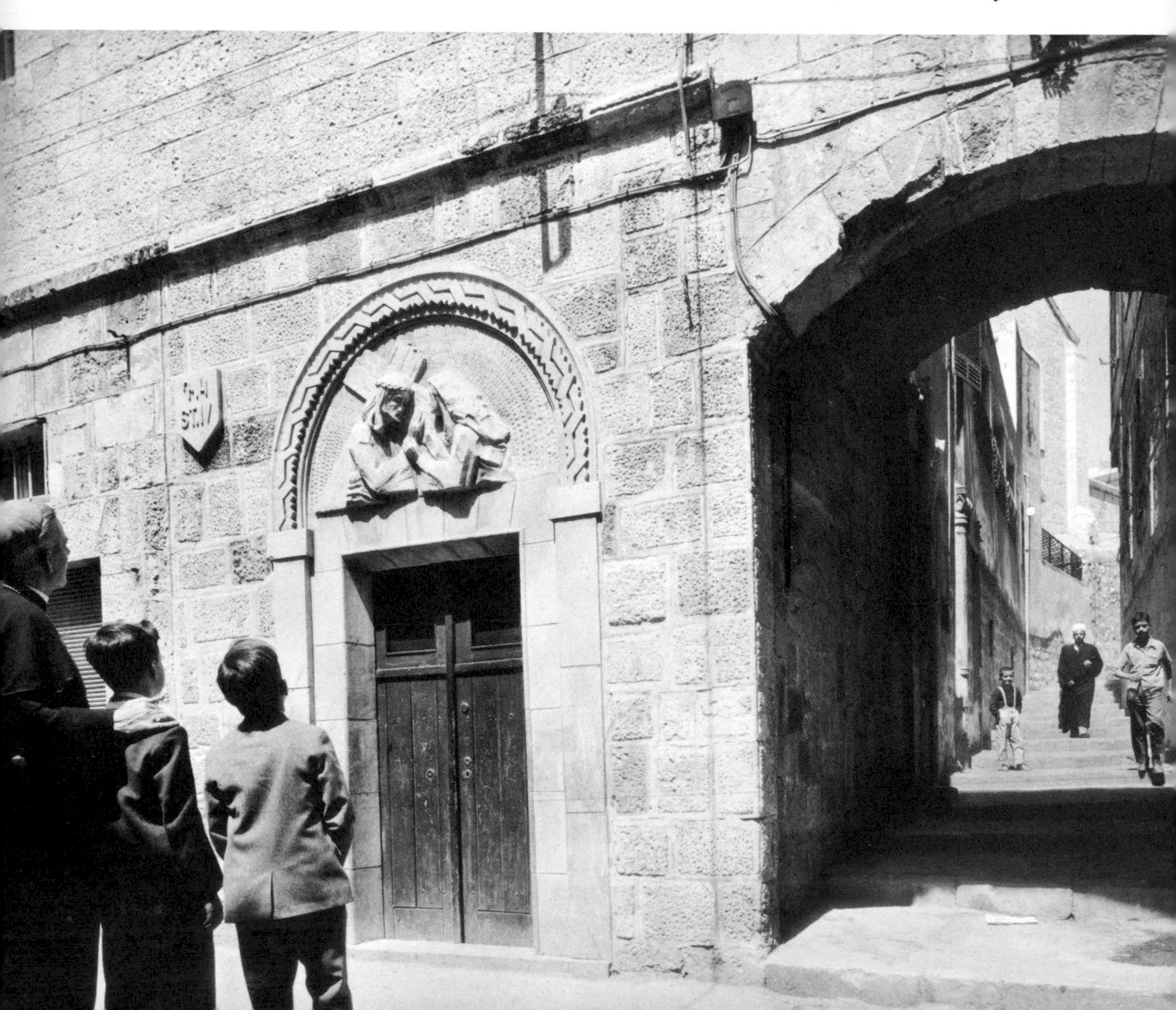

VI THE TOMB OF CHRIST

The Basilica of the Holy Sepulchre, as built by Constantine the Great and consecrated in the year A.D. 336, was one of the most beautiful and unusual churches the world has seen; today it is the most painful spectacle in the Holy Land. When seen first by the Crusaders in the eleventh century, seven hundred years of disaster and reconstruction had already obliterated all traces of the original plan, and the conquerors of the Holy Land were distressed to see a shrine which looked to them unworthy of its sanctity. Since then its history has been one of steady disintegration, culminating in 1927 in an earthquake which threatened to bring down the entire building.

This was a wonderful opportunity to create a worthy church upon the most sacred spot in Christendom, but the state of pious catalepsy engendered by divided ownership resulted in merely supporting the structure with steel girders and enormous beams of timber, inside and out. During the fighting in Jerusalem in 1948, mortar fire still further threatened the building with collapse; but nothing was done except to increase the steel and timber. Now—thirty-three years after the earthquake—the venerable structure is still theoretically held together by supports which actually, in contraction and expansion during the heat of the Palestinian summer, are pulling apart what they were erected to protect.

The Franciscans have prepared a plan for the rebuilding of the Church, which would restore to it something of the dignity and clarity of the Constantinian basilica, but the various communities have agreed only on a $1,400,000 restoration, on the understanding that nothing is to be altered.

INRI

To understand what an opportunity is being lost, it is necessary to have some idea what the church looked like when it left the hands of Constantine's architects. It was a companion basilica to the first St. Peter's in Rome, and should be considered together with that building. When Constantine decided to reveal the tomb of St. Peter for the veneration of the faithful, his engineers were faced with a mighty problem. The Vatican Hill slopes from north to south and in order to enshrine the tomb in front of the apse of the church, it was necessary to cut away a great section of the hill to make a level platform. This was done in the short time of seven years. Taking the tomb of St. Peter as ground level, everything else was cut away over the enormous area to be covered by the church, and a beautiful basilica was erected, approached by a wide flight of steps leading into an atrium open to the sky. This led into the majestic basilica, where, at the west end (all the Constantinian churches faced the east), the tomb of the Apostle rose from the pavement.

After this church had been built, or while it was building, Constantine decided to employ the same technique in Jerusalem. The tradition that the Tomb of Christ and Calvary were concealed beneath the enormous rotunda on which Hadrian had erected a temple of Venus was one known to every Christian in Jerusalem. These two places were close together. "In the same quarter where he was crucified there was a garden, with a new tomb in it . . ."[8] When the temple was demolished the architects were faced, not with a more or less tractable hill, but with a mass of rock, and with two sites, instead of one, to be enshrined: the Tomb of St. Joseph of Arimathea and Calvary.

Employing the same methods as on the Vatican Hill, they took the threshold of the Tomb as their ground level and cut away all the surrounding rock, leaving the Tomb standing up alone, and, nearby, the rock of Calvary was cut down to a convenient size. Round the tomb was erected a graceful rotunda and Calvary was left in the open air, surrounded by a beautiful colonnade. Eastward of Calvary was built the basilica and the entrance atrium. So the original Church of the Holy Sepulchre was composed of four sections skilfully linked together: first, the entrance steps leading to the atrium with its fountain;

Chapel of the Nailing to the Cross, Church of the Holy Sepulchre, Jerusalem

then the noble basilica, divided into five naves by four rows of marble columns; then the Rock of Calvary in its open colonnades; and, finally, the Rotunda, in the center of which rose the Tomb of Christ.

This exquisite and unique building led the pilgrim by solemn stages to the crown of his pilgrimage. The earliest travelers have described how, after passing through the basilica, they came into the open air and saw Calvary standing in its courtyard, surrounded by a silver balustrade and surmounted by a richly decorated cross. From this atrium, a door led into the Rotunda, in the center of which the rough limestone Tomb of Christ was to be seen. St. Cyril of Jerusalem (386) said that in his time the millstone, which was rolled in place to close the Tomb, was still to be seen there; Arculf, at the end of the seventh century, noticed marks of the chisels on the Tomb, "on the white limestone veined with red." In 1112, the Abbot Daniel was the first to mention that the tomb was covered with marble, with three openings through which the pilgrim could touch and kiss the rock.

The history of this lovely church is one of destruction and humiliation. The glorious clarity of its design has long since been lost, and the eastern end of the basilica is now covered by the Khan al-Zeit, where, among the bazaars, may be found traces of the great Constantinian entrance doorway.[9] It was this truncated church which the Crusaders did their best to improve. Then followed centuries of Moslem occupation, in which the old building continued to fall to pieces and to be shaken by earthquakes. In 1808, when Europe was engaged in the Napoleonic Wars, a fire damaged the church, and the Greeks obtained a firman from the Sultan of Turkey authorizing them to repair the building, which was done with unhappy results. The architect from Mitylene, whom they employed, laid down a new Stone of Unction and destroyed the tombs of the Latin Kings of Jerusalem. His worst offense was to erect above the Tomb of Christ the unfortunate structure to be seen there today, which has neither beauty nor antiquity to recommend it.

It is, however, odd, but true, that the very factors which have produced the present plight of this fabric demand one's respect. The guardians of the Tomb have remained at their posts through centuries of oppression, ready, if need be, to shed their blood in its defense. The

Entrance, Holy Sepulchre, Church of the Holy Sepulchre, Jerusalem

ΜΥΡΟΦΟΡΟΙ ΓΥΝΑΙΚΕΣ· Τ ΖΗΤΕΙΤΕ ΤΟΝ ΖΩΝΤΑ ΕΝ ΝΕΚΡΟΙΣ ΑΝΕΣΗ

red tides of history have often washed against the building, and have even lapped the very tomb of God. There have been times when only the most intense devotion has kept the tapers burning there, and maintained the long chain of prayer and supplication. It is perhaps not strange when we reflect that resistance to disaster, which has been the main factor in the preservation of this holy place, should have induced in the minds of those who have protected it so long, a condition of mind which suspects change as something also to be resisted.

One's first impression of the Church of the Holy Sepulchre is sadly different from that of the fortunate ones who saw it in all the noble clarity of its original design. Now one sees a dark warren where gloomy flights of steps lead here and there into the heart of a pious labyrinth. Eastern priests, square-bearded like Assyrian kings, chant their litanies at altars blazing with color and encrusted with gold and silver. One comes to the austere Latin Chapel on Calvary with a sense of having returned home.

The Tomb of our Lord is approached by a little marble vestibule called the Chapel of the Angel, because it was here that the Angel told the weeping women that Christ had risen. The Tomb beyond is a space only seven feet long by five feet wide, also entirely encased in marble, where a Greek priest stands ready to give tapers to those who come to pray. There is room for two, or at the most, three, people in the small space to the right where, three feet above the floor, a slab of marble covers the Tomb of Christ.

"And at very early dawn on the first day of the week they came to the tomb, bringing the spices they had prepared: and found the stone already rolled away from the door of the tomb. They went into it, and could not find the body of the Lord Jesus. They were still puzzling over this, when two men came and stood by them, in shining garments. These said to them, as they bowed their faces to the earth in fear, Why are you seeking one who is alive, here among the dead? He is not here, he has risen again; remember how he told you, while he was still in Galilee."[10]

Holy Sepulchre, Church of the Holy Sepulchre, Jerusalem

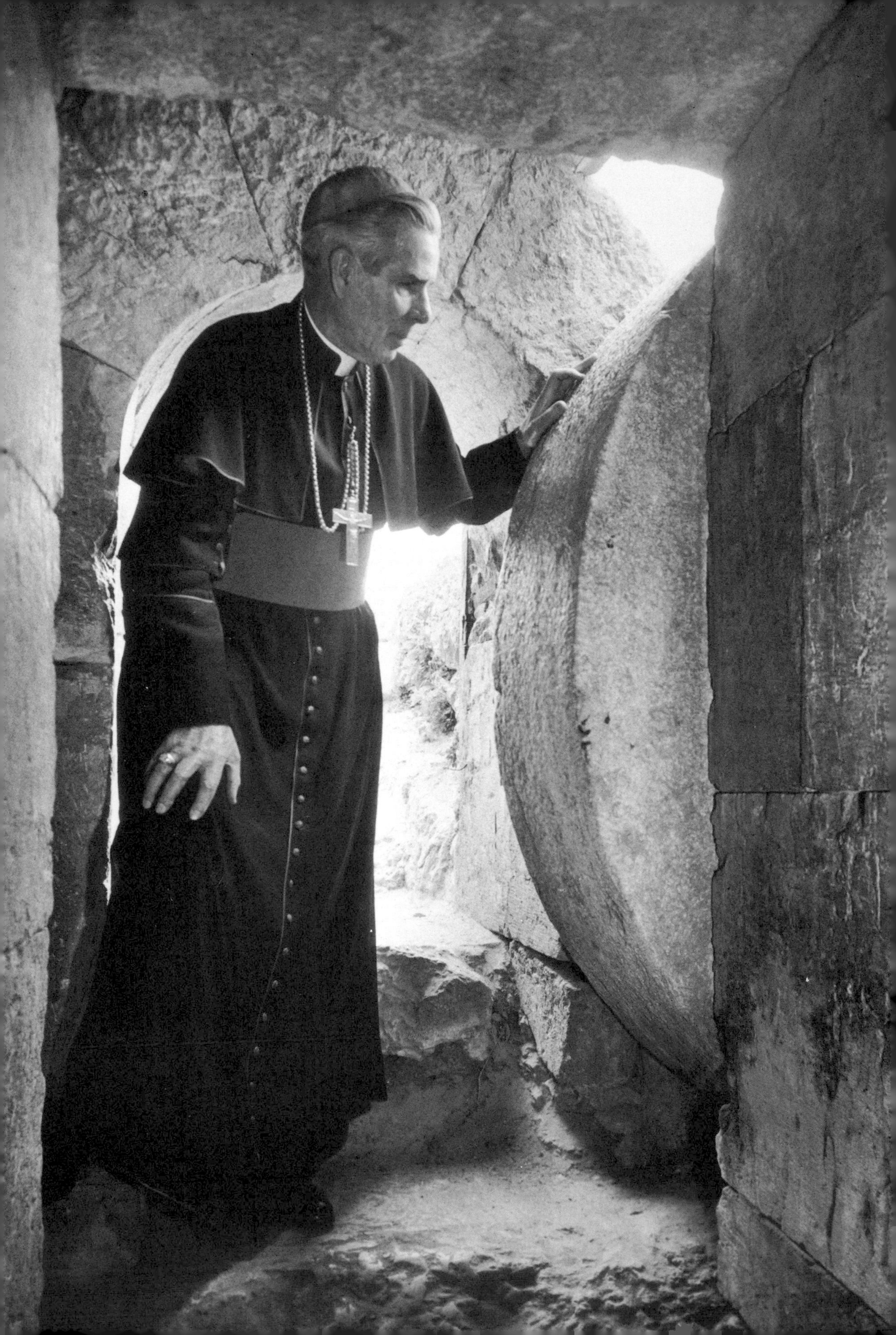

AN AFTERWORD

by Bishop Sheen

SIX MONTHS after the pilgrimage was over I asked Fulton and Jerry what impressed them most deeply in all that they saw in the Holy Land.

Fulton said, "Calvary and the Via Dolorosa."

Jerry said, "The Holy Sepulchre."

Now of all these scenes in the Holy Land, these are the two with which adults most generally express disappointment—because they are not as they were then, or because of the tensions existing between the Latins and the Greeks, or because the Holy Sepulchre is old.

But the faith of each of the boys stripped off the quarrels and the bickerings of centuries, quickly excavated the layers of history and came back to the fundamental of all fundamentals.

Fulton had a preference for death; Jerry had a preference for life. When I asked the reason for the choice of each, Fulton answered, "If Our Lord had not died on Calvary for our sins, we would not be redeemed."

The answer of Jerry was: "But the Resurrection was the proof of His victory over sin."

I was pleased to receive those answers, for they are one. Calvary was the greatest act of love the world ever knew. Our Lord never

Typical millstone used to seal a tomb, Herodian Tomb, Jerusalem spoke of His Passion and His Death without speaking of His Resurrection. The answer of the boys was like a coin with two sides; one bearing the act of love, the other bearing the act of victory.

Whenever I wish to review my catechism and the great mystery of life, I shall go back to Fulton and Jerry and discover they know more than the "wise and prudent of this world"—for without a Good Friday one could never have an Easter Sunday; without the Cross, there could never have been the empty tomb.

Back at school with souvenirs

NOTES

1 THE HOLY PLACES

[1] Eusebius: *Hist. Eccles.*, 6:20.
[2] Acts, 10:1-8.
[3] III Kings, 13:1-34.
[4] *Palestine Pilgrims' Text Society*, Vol. I, pp. 23-4.
[5] Jerome: *Ep.* CVIII.
[6] Pal. Pil. Text Soc., Vol. 11.
[7] *The Holy Land and the Franciscans*, Franciscan Press, Jerusalem.

2 THE COMING

[1] Thomas de Celano: *Life of St. Francis of Assisi.*
[2] William of Chartres.
[3] Luke, 1:36-37.
[4] Jerome: *Ep.* CVIII.
[5] Edersheim, A.: *The Life and Times of Jesus the Messiah*, Vol. I.
[6] Butcher, E. L.: *The Story of the Church in Egypt*, p. 7.
[7] Acts, 7:22.

3 THE MINISTRY

[1] Ronald Cox in his commentary to *The Gospel Story.*
[2] Luke, 3:23.
[3] Matt., 3:13.
[4] Sheen, Fulton J.: *Life of Christ*, p. 50.
[5] *Pal. Pil. Text Soc.*, Vol. V, p. 48.
[6] Jeremias, 32:14.
[7] Sheen, Fulton J.: *Life of Christ*, p. 103.
[8] *Patrologiae cursus completus*, Greek Series, 117/359.
[9] Matt., 26:73.
[10] Morton, H. V.: *In the Steps of the Master*, p. 178.
[11] Matt., 9:1.
[12] Matt., 9:35.
[13] Mark, 4:11.
[14] Luke, 7:1-5.
[15] John, 6:35-6, 49-52, 54-57.
[16] John, 6:70-72.
[17] Withycombe, E. G.: *The Oxford Dictionary of English Christian Names*, p. 200.
[18] Perkins, W. and J. Toynbee: *The Shrine of St. Peter*, pp. 116-7.
[19] Guarducci, M.: *The Tomb of St. Peter*, p. 142.
[20] John, 21:1-14.
[21] Sheen, Fulton J.: *Life of Christ*, pp. 125-6.
[22] Votaw, C. W.: In *Sermon on the Mount* in Hastings' *Dictionary of the Bible*, extra vol., pp. 14-5.
[23] *Pal. Pil. Text. Soc.*, Vol. 111.
[24] Psalms, 88:13.
[25] Luke, 9:33-36.
[26] Matt., 17:2.
[27] Luke, 9:44.

4 THE WAY OF THE CROSS

[1] Hoade, E.: *The Place of the Last Supper and the Tomb of David*, Franciscan Press, Jerusalem.
[2] Luke, 22:15-22.
[3] Mark, 14:34.
[4] John, 6:1-5.
[5] Mark, 15:16.
[6] John, 19-13.
[7] *Le Lithostrotos*, Dillen & Cie, Paris.
[8] John, 19:41.
[9] Harvey, W.: *Church of the Holy Sepulchre, Jerusalem. Structural Survey. Final Report*, 1935.
[10] Luke, 24:1-7.

(*All references to chapters and verses of The Holy Bible are to the translation by Ronald Knox.*)

A FOOTNOTE ON ANTONIO BARLUZZI

As THIS book goes to press, Antonio Barluzzi, the architect whose churches are so often mentioned in its pages, lies critically ill in Rome. He is seventy-six years of age and has devoted the greater part of his life to the shrines of the Holy Land.

Born in Rome in 1884, he studied architecture and engineering at the University of Rome, and before the First World War had designed, in collaboration with his brother, Giulio, several notable buildings in Italy and Palestine. In 1918, the Father Custos asked him to build the churches of Gethsemane and Mount Tabor, but Barluzzi, who believed he had a vocation for the Church, begged for time. He hurried to Rome and consulted the confessor of his youth. "Go and build the shrines and then we can talk," said the priest. Barluzzi commented in his diary: "My heart leapt for joy and I said 'God wills it.' I returned forthwith to Jerusalem."

First with his brother, then alone, Barluzzi devoted his life (he was then thirty-four) to the building of the chief shrines. He lived with the Franciscans as a Franciscan, attending Mass every day, joining the friars for meditation and participating in the devotional exercises. Those who know him do not hesitate to describe him as "saintly." In a letter to the General of the Franciscan Order written in 1934, Barluzzi defined his work as "a tendency to translate by architecture the majesty and simplicity of the Bible . . . work executed with the enthusiasm of a mission."

After the consecration of the churches at Gethsemane and Mount Tabor in 1924, he received a gold Pontifical medal. Though his contribution to the church architecture of the Holy Land is greater than that of any other man, and though he has received eleven decorations for his distinguished work, his name does not appear in any Italian or international book of reference. In addition to the two churches already mentioned, his chief works include the Church of the Good Shepherd, Jericho (1924-25); restoration of the Latin Chapel on Calvary (1933-37); the Church of the Beatitudes, Galilee (1936-38); the Church of the Visitation at Ain Karem (begun 1938, interrupted by World War II, completed 1950); the Church of St. Lazarus, Bethany (1952-54); the Chapel of the Shepherds, Bethlehem (1952-54); and the Dominus Flevit (1955). In addition, he has designed and built many convents, schools and hospitals.

In 1941, he produced with Luigi Marangoni, and under the inspiration of the Apostolic Delegate, Msgr. (now Cardinal) Testa, the ambitious plan for a new Church of the Holy Sepulchre. This was published in Bergamo.

As early as 1940, he was conceiving a plan for the rebuilding of the great basilica at Nazareth, a church that was to crown all his achievements. In 1958, a blow fell which was to shatter his health and, as one who knows him well says, "to break his heart." His design for the basilica at Nazareth was rejected. That same night, Barluzzi had a severe heart attack, which led to cerebral deafness and emphysema. He was seventy-four years old and penniless, having given all his money away. In his sickness and despair, he went to Rome and sought refuge with his lifelong friends, the Franciscans, at the Terra Sancta Delegation near the Lateran. In a bare cell containing only a bed, a chair, a table and a crucifix, the great architect has lingered since that time; and to his other physical trials have been added loss of memory and partial blindness.

Father Eugene Hoade, so well known in Palestine and now of the Padri Penitenzieri Lateranensi, to whom I am indebted for the above information, took me to see Barluzzi in May, 1960, but warned me that he would probably be unaware of our presence. This proved to be so. I found the experience harrowing. When in health and standing upright, Barluzzi must have been a commanding and impressive figure, a man at least six feet in height with a finely cut profile and a mass of iron-gray hair. Now, lean to the point of emaciation, he bears upon his features all the marks of ill-health and self-crucifixion. I thought he resembled nothing so much as a saint by El Greco.

H.V.M.

INDEX

(Prepared by Elsa Wagner Nugent)

ABOUT THIS BOOK AND THE MEN WHO MADE IT

FULTON JOHN SHEEN was born May 8, 1895, at El Paso, Illinois, one of four sons of Newton Morris and Delia (Fulton) Sheen. He was baptized Peter and took the name John at confirmation, later adopting his mother's maiden name. His father was a farmer, but the family later moved to Peoria, Ill., where he attended St. Mary's School and Spalding Institute, from which he was graduated in 1913. He received his A.B. and M.A. degrees from St. Viator College, Bourbonnais, Ill., where he first tasted the pleasures of speaking and writing as a member of the college debating team and newspaper staff. He completed his theological studies at St. Paul's Seminary, St. Paul, Minn., and was ordained to the priesthood for the Diocese of Peoria, September 20, 1919. A year later he obtained his degrees of Bachelor of Sacred Theology and Bachelor of Canon Law from the Catholic University of America, and went to the University of Louvain, Belgium, where he was awarded a Ph.D. in 1923. He also attended the Sorbonne in Paris and the Collegio Angelico in Rome. In 1924 he received his Doctorate of Sacred Theology in Rome, and a year later while teaching dogmatic theology at St. Edmund's College, Ware, England, he was made an *Agrégé en Philosophie* by Louvain and awarded that university's Cardinal Mercier International Philosophy Award. His honorary degrees include LL.D., Litt.D. and L.H.D. On his return to the United States, he served as a curate of St. Patrick's Church in Peoria and joined the faculty of the Catholic University of America, Washington, D.C., in 1926 as a philosophy of religion instructor, later being promoted to a full professorship. In June, 1934, he was appointed Papal Chamberlain and was elevated the following year to Domestic Prelate. He was consecrated Bishop on June 11, 1951, a year after he became National Director of the Society for the Propagation of the Faith. As a preacher he has been heard by millions in the United States, Canada and England, through the media of radio and television. A prolific writer, he is author of two syndicated columns: "God Love You" for the Catholic press, and "Bishop Sheen Speaks," for the secular press; and is editor of two magazines: World-mission, a quarterly review, and Mission, a bi-monthly. The popularity of his radio and television programs can be judged from the fact that his daily mail as a result of these programs has reached as much as ten thousand letters in a single day—about one-third of them from non-Catholics. The largest single delivery of mail after a program was thirty thousand letters. He conducted the first religious service ever telecast, served as narrator for a March of Time film, and has had his sermons issued in record album form. His interests are wide, and as well as serving in such organizations as the Catholic Literary Guild and the American Catholic Philosophical Society, he is an active member of the Mediaeval Academy and the American Geographical Association. The long list of his books started with publication of *God and Intelligence in Modern Philosophy* (Longmans, Green, 1925). This was followed by *Religion Without God* (Longmans, Green, 1928), *The Life of All Living* (Century, 1929), *The Divine Romance* (Century, 1930), *Old Errors and New Labels* (Century, 1931), *Moods and Truths* (Century, 1932), *The Way of the Cross* (Appleton-Century, 1933), *Seven Last Words* (Appleton-Century, 1933), *The Eternal Galilean* (Appleton-Century, 1934), *The Philosophy of Science* (Bruce, 1934), *The Mystical Body of Christ* (Sheed and Ward, 1935), *Calvary and the Mass* (Kenedy, 1936), *The Moral Universe* (Bruce, 1936), *The Cross and the Beatitudes* (Kenedy, 1937), *The Cross and the Crisis* (Bruce, 1938), *Liberty, Equality and Fraternity* (Macmillan, 1938), *The Rainbow of Sorrow* (Kenedy, 1938), *Victory Over Vice* (Kenedy, 1939), *Freedom Under God* (Bruce, 1940), *Whence Come Wars* (Sheed and Ward, 1940), *The Seven Virtues* (Kenedy, 1940), *For God and Country* (Kenedy, 1941), *A Declaration of Dependence* (Bruce, 1941), *God and War* (Kenedy, 1942), *The Divine Verdict* (Kenedy, 1943), *The Armor of God* (Kenedy, 1943), *Philosophies at War* (Scribner's, 1943), *Seven Words to the Cross* (Kenedy, 1944), *Seven Pillars of Peace* (Scribner's, 1944), *Love*

Left to right: Mr. Karsh, Bishop Sheen and Mr. Morton on Mount Sion, Jerusalem

One Another (Kenedy, 1944), *Seven Words of Jesus and Mary* (Kenedy, 1945), *Preface to Religion* (Kenedy, 1946), *Characters of the Passion* (Kenedy, 1946), *Jesus, Son of Mary* (McMullen, 1947), *Communism and the Conscience of the West* (Bobbs, Merrill, 1948), *Philosophy of Religion* (Appleton-Century-Crofts, 1948), *Peace of Soul* (McGraw-Hill, 1949), *Lift Up Your Heart* (McGraw-Hill, 1950), *Three to Get Married* (Appleton-Century Crofts, 1951), *The World's First Love* (McGraw-Hill, 1952), *Life Is Worth Living, First Series* (McGraw-Hill, 1953), *Life Is Worth Living, Second Series* (McGraw-Hill, 1954), *The Life of Christ* (McGraw-Hill, 1954), *The Way to Happiness* (Garden City, 1954), *Life Is Worth Living, Third Series* (McGraw-Hill, 1955), *The Way to Inner Peace* (Garden City, 1955), *God Love You* (Garden City, 1955), *Thinking Life Through* (Garden City, 1955), *The True Meaning of Christmas* (McGraw-Hill, 1955), *Life Is Worth Living, Fourth Series* (McGraw-Hill, 1956), *Thoughts for Daily Living* (Garden City, 1956), *Life Is Worth Living, Fifth Series* (McGraw-Hill, 1957), *This Is the Mass* (Hawthorn, 1958), *This Is Rome* (Hawthorn, 1960) and *Go to Heaven* (McGraw-Hill, 1960). He is Auxiliary Bishop of New York.

YOUSUF KARSH was born December 23, 1908, at Mardin, Armenia, and left for Canada at the age of fifteen during the Turkish massacres. Son of an import-export entrepreneur and grandson of an engraver, he went to stay with an uncle, A. G. Nakash, who owned a photography studio in Sherbrooke, Quebec. He took an interest in the art of the camera and was sent by his uncle to Boston to study. After several years in the United States he went to open his own studio in Canada's capital, where within a few years he was photographing the cream of society and leaders of government. When war broke out in 1939, Ottawa became a center of Allied war activity and "Karsh of Ottawa" became a familiar signature on the portraits of some of the world's greatest leaders. His famous portrait of Winston Churchill in 1941 rocketed him to fame as the world's greatest portrait photographer, and that photograph, along with seventy-four others, taken in all parts of the world in the four years that followed, went into making his first book, *Faces of Destiny* (Ziff-Davis, 1946). He followed this with *This Is the Mass* (Hawthorn, 1958), *Portraits of Greatness* (Thomas Nelson & Sons, 1959) and *This is Rome* (Hawthorn, 1960). Still a world traveler, he keeps cameras and equipment at studios in London, Paris and New York, as well as in Ottawa, and usually carries a set of traveling equipment that weighs a minimum of 250 pounds. He always uses a white camera, finding that the traditional black is too depressing, and his focusing cloth varies in color with his own mood—though it is most often of red velvet with a gold satin lining. Groups of his portraits form part of the permanent collections of such museums as the Brooklyn Museum Department of Photography and the Museum of Modern Art in New York, Eastman House, Rochester, N.Y., The Art Institute of Chicago, and the Huntington Library, San Marino, Cal. In acknowledgment of his contribution to Canadian art and culture he received one of the first Canadian Citizenship Certificates in January, 1947, when Parliament passed a law creating Canadian citizenship. He is actively interested in Canadian theatre and met Solange Gauthier, whom he married in 1939, when she was acting with the Ottawa Drama League. She serves frequently as model for his work and shares his love for gardening and tennis.

H. V. MORTON, author and traveler, was born in England in 1892. He has been called the "world's greatest travel writer." At the age of nineteen he became Assistant Editor on the Birmingham *Gazette and Express*. He then went to the London *Daily Mail* where he stayed until the outbreak of World War I. After four years in the Royal Army he returned to England and began to explore the British Isles. He started with a study of England and its people which was published as *In Search of England*. Then came Scotland in *In Search of Scotland*. *In Search of Ireland* gave the flavor of the Emerald Isle. He became an honorary "bard" for *In Search of Wales*. Mr. Morton next turned his attention to the land where Christianity first began. *In the Steps of the Master* recounted a trip that followed the journeyings of Jesus in the Holy Land. He next followed the path of the three missionary journeys of the Apostle Paul in his *In the Steps of St. Paul*. His masterpiece of biblical history, *The Lands of the Bible*, was a travel narrative of a trip through all the ancient lands mentioned in the Bible—Babylon, Egypt, the Holy Land, the sites of the ancient kingdoms and empires in the time of biblical events. Going on to new adventures, he is now writing of European countries and has completed books on Spain and Italy. He is the author of *The Heart of London* (1925), *London* (1926), *The London Year* (1926), *The Spell of London* (1926), *The Nights of London* (1926), *In Search of England* (Dodd, Mead, 1927), *The Call of England* (Dodd, Mead, 1928), *In Search of Scotland* (Dodd, Mead, 1930), *In Search of Ireland* (Dodd, Mead, 1931), *In Search of Wales* (Dodd, Mead, 1932), *Blue Days at Sea* (Dodd, Mead, 1932), *In Scotland Again* (Dodd, Mead, 1933), *In the Steps of the Master* (Dodd, Mead, 1934), *The London Scene* (Dodd, Mead, 1935), *Our Fellow Men* (Dodd, Mead, 1936), *In the Steps of St. Paul* (Dodd, Mead, 1936), *The Lands of the Bible* (Dodd, Mead, 1938), *Ghosts of London* (Dodd, Mead, 1939), *In Search of the Northern Isles* (1940), *Women of the Bible* (1940), *Middle East* (1941), *I, James Blunt* (1942), *Morton's London* (Dodd, Mead, 1950), *Stranger in Spain* (Dodd, Mead, 1954), *Traveller in Rome* (Dodd, Mead, 1957), and *This is Rome* (Hawthorn, 1960). He lives in Somerset West, Union of South Africa.

THIS IS THE HOLY LAND (Hawthorn, 1961) was designed by Ernst Reichl. The body type is *Caledonia*, designed for the Linotype by W. A. Dwiggins, and was set by the Atlantic Linotype Co., Inc., Brooklyn. The type face used for the chapter numbers, titles and initials is *Solemnis*, designed in Berlin by G. G. Lange. The text and the black and white illustrations were printed by Edward Stern and Co., Inc., in Philadelphia, using the Optakrome process, on White Rose Vellum stock, which was manufactured by the P. H. Glatfelter Co., Spring Grove, Pennsylvania. The four-color section was printed by Publishers Printing–Rogers Kellogg Corp. of Long Island City, New York. The book was bound by the Montauk Book Manufacturing Co., Inc., New York City.

A HAWTHORN BOOK

915.694
M846
120076

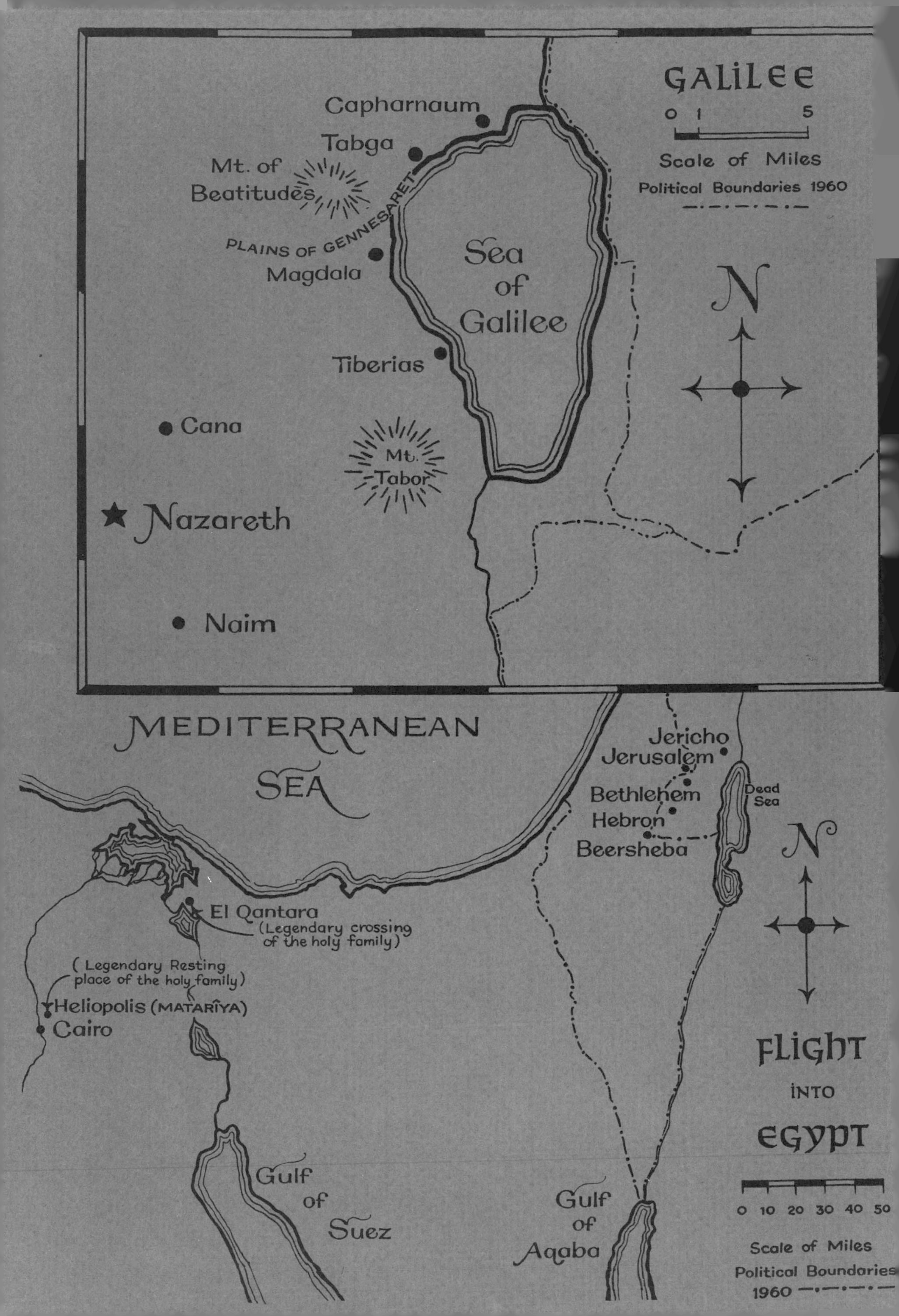
GALILEE
0 1 5
Scale of Miles
Political Boundaries 1960
Capharnaum
Tabga
Mt. of Beatitudes
PLAINS OF GENNESARET
Magdala
Sea of Galilee
Tiberias
N
Cana
Mt. Tabor
Nazareth
Naim
MEDITERRANEAN SEA
Jericho
Jerusalem
Bethlehem
Hebron
Beersheba
Dead Sea
N
El Qantara
(Legendary crossing of the holy family)
(Legendary Resting place of the holy family)
Heliopolis (MATARÎYA)
Cairo
FLIGHT INTO EGYPT
0 10 20 30 40 50
Scale of Miles
Political Boundaries 1960
Gulf of Suez
Gulf of Aqaba